ICT SKILL FOR LIFE

ICT SKILL FOR LIFE

ALAN CLARKE

Hodder Arnold

A MEMBER OF THE HODDER HEADLINE GROUP

Orders: please contact Bookpoint Ltd, 130 Milton Park, Abingdon, Oxon OX14 4SB. Telephone: (44) 01235 827720. Fax: (44) 01235 400454. Lines are open from 9.00–5.00, Monday to Saturday, with a 24 hour message answering service. You can also order through our website www.hoddereducation.co.uk

If you have any comments to make about this, or any of our other titles, please send them to educationenquiries@hodder.co.uk

British Library Cataloguing in Publication Data
A catalogue record for this title is available from the British Library

ISBN-13: 978 0 340 941 553

Published 2007
Impression number   10 9 8 7 6 5 4 3 2 1
Year   2009 2008 2007

Hodder Headline's policy is to use papers that are natural, renewable and recyclable products and made from wood grown in sustainable forests. The logging and manufacturing processes are expected to conform to the environmental regulations of the country of origin.

Cover photo from Dick White/Digital Vision/Getty Images.
Typeset by Pantek Arts Ltd, Maidstone Kent.
Printed in Great Britain for Hodder & Stoughton Educational, a division of Hodder Headline Plc, 338 Euston Road, London NW1 3BH by CPI Bath.

Acknowledgements

The author and publisher wish to acknowledge Microsoft Corporation, NIACE and Prudential, Wikipedia and Google for the use of the screen capture images.

Screen capture shots are reprinted with permission from Microsoft Corporation.

The information and exercises in this book are based on Microsoft Windows Professional XP® operating system and Microsoft Office 2003®.

CONTENTS

1 Introduction

In 2004, the UK government decided that information and communication technologies (ICTs) were essential skills. That is, they are essential in a similar way to reading, writing and number work. These types of essential skills are called 'Skills for Life'. The government made the decision because:

1. The majority of new and existing jobs require information and communication technology (ICT) skills.
2. Technology is part of everyone's life.
3. Computers are an important aspect of education and training.
4. Many government and commercial services are available online.

You may want to learn to send emails, use a digital camera, word-process a letter, shop online or plan a holiday. There is a vast range of possibilities. You need to study to meet your own needs.

You may already have used some technology such as a mobile phone or a cash machine. This provides a starting point to develop your skills. At the beginning of the course you may not be aware of all the possibilities. You will perhaps want to explore different devices and applications.

Vocab

In this context, **explore** means to try different options to see what they do.

An **application** is a tool on the computer that allows you to carry out different tasks. A word-processing application helps you to write and present text.

What is information and communication technology?

Information and communication technology (ICT) covers a wide range of technologies and uses. The Skill for Life allows you a lot of freedom about which technologies to study. The choice depends on your needs. The Skill for Life standard expects people to use technology as part of their:

1. Work
2. Home life
3. Education
4. Community activities
5. Free time.

The ICT Skill for Life standard gives the above five areas specific names. These are as follows:

1. Community activities: citizen and community
2. Work: economic activity, including paid and unpaid work
3. Home life: domestic and everyday life
4. Free time: leisure
5. Education: education and training.

The above terms are used throughout the book so that you know how the tasks you are studying relate to the areas.

What is ICT Skill for Life?

A standard has been agreed for ICT as a Skill for Life. This standard is presented in five levels:

- Entry Level 1
- Entry Level 2
- Entry Level 3
- Level 1
- Level 2.

Entry Level 1 is for beginners who have never used any ICT, while Level 2 is the equivalent of a GCSE qualification. You start to learn at the level appropriate to you and then progress through the levels.

To help teachers and trainers to deliver the standard, a national curriculum document has been designed. The curriculum provides an explanation of the standard and many examples of what it covers.

Qualifications have been developed based on the standards and are offered at the different levels. This book covers three of the Entry Level qualifications.

Purposeful

The ICT Skill for Life standard requires that it is taught in a purposeful way. This means that it meets your needs. You may have many reasons for wanting to use ICT, and it helps to consider these reasons. The standard provides five groups of reasons:

1. Citizen and community. For example, to help you read the local council website in order to find out how council tax is being spent.
2. Economic activity, including paid and unpaid work. For example, to help you to write a letter to a customer.
3. Domestic and everyday life. For example, to help you learn to take digital photographs while on holiday.
4. Leisure. For example, to help you to plan a trip.
5. Education and training. For example, to help your children complete an assignment for school.

The practical tasks in each chapter are grouped together under these headings so that you can select those that are relevant to you.

At the moment, you may not be completely certain about what you want to learn. If this is the case, you can consider the different options. You may wish to do this anyway to see how you can use ICT in other parts of your life.

Practical tasks

The ICT Skill for Life standard describes ICT skills and knowledge under three main headings:

1. Using ICT systems – this focuses on using the equipment such as printers, digital cameras and computers.
2. Finding and exchanging information – this centres on using the internet and communication technologies such as email.
3. Developing and presenting information – this aims to create materials using tools such as word processors.

The three groups do overlap. For instance, you need to be able to use the equipment to create a document on a word processor; by exchanging information, you will create new text; and the reason for using a computer is often to find information on the World Wide Web – the internet.

The practical tasks within this book are linked to specific headings, for example 'Using ICT systems'. However, they will often help in the other areas such as 'Developing and presenting information'.

Examples for 'Finding and exchanging information' and 'Developing and presenting information' practical task headings and descriptions, respectively:

ICT Skill for Life standard

This task helps you to practise:

■ recognising and using appropriate sources of ICT

■ using ICT to communicate.

ICT Skill for Life standard

This task helps you to practise:

■ entering information and editing it

■ checking content and correcting errors

■ presenting information that is fit for a purpose.

Qualifications

The ICT Skill for Life standard has been used as the basis to design qualifications. This book covers some of the qualifications for Entry Levels 1 to 3. Three major awarding bodies have developed qualifications:

- OCR
- City and Guilds
- Edexcel.

You may be studying for any of these ICT Skill for Life Entry Level qualifications. This book covers the standard and the qualifications from these three awarding bodies. Other bodies have also produced awards but these are not included in this book.

2 Entry Level 1: Introducing ICT

Objectives

This chapter will help you to:

- use ICT systems:
    - use ICT for a purpose
    - recognise and use interface features
    - follow recommended safe practices.
- find and exchange information:
    - recognise sources of information
    - get simple information from an ICT-based source that matches requirements
    - receive ICT-based communication.
- develop and present information:
    - enter and edit simple information
    - identify and correct simple errors
    - submit information.

> ## Vocab
>
> **Interface features** are the objects shown on the screen.
>
> **Requirements** has several meanings. In this case, it means your own needs.
>
> **Edit** means to make changes, for example to change the spelling of a word.

Assumptions

At Entry Level 1 it is assumed that:

- you will need help and support
- the computer or other ICT equipment has been switched on and made ready for you to use
- the applications have already been loaded and are ready for you to use.

Qualifications

This chapter will help you if you are studying for a qualification awarded by:

- OCR
- City and Guilds
- Edexcel.

Practical tasks

This section contains a variety of tasks. They allow you to practise many of the skills required in Entry Level 1 and to improve your understanding of ICT. You can do the tasks in any order, and it is not necessary to complete them all.

Citizen and community

1. Use a cash machine

ICT Skill for Life standard

This task helps you to practise:

- using ICT for a purpose
- recognising and using interface features
- entering and editing simple information
- submitting information.

Vocab

Enter Enter has several meanings. In this case, it means typing in information using the keyboard.

Submit means to send. In this case, you send information to the computer system so that it can act. Usually you press or click on a button.

PIN is your Personal Identification Number for your credit or debit card.

There are many times when you need to operate a cash machine. You may want to withdraw cash, obtain a statement of your account, or change your PIN number.

a. Use a cash machine for your bank or building society by inserting your card and entering your PIN number.

b. Read the display. Try to identify all the different options and symbols used to show the purpose of a key or to display an item. Figure 2.1 shows an example of a cash machine display.

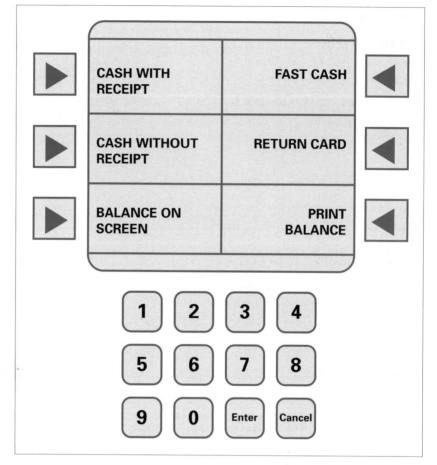

Figure 2.1 Cash machine

c. Complete a task, such as withdrawing cash, by selecting from the different options and following the instructions.

d. When you have finished, exit the system in the correct way by following the displayed instructions.

Vocab

Exit means to leave. In this case, it means to leave the system by removing your card and cash.

Extra task

Use several different cash machines over a period of time and compare what each displays. Are they all identical? You may see that symbols vary and that the layout of the interface display changes.

Vocab

Interface display This is what appears on the screen.

2. Use a credit or debit card

ICT Skill for Life standard

This task helps you to practise:

■ using ICT for a purpose

■ recognising and using interface features

■ entering simple information

■ submitting information.

Paying for products and services using a credit or debit card is now a normal part of the way we live. Modern cards use chip and PIN. This is where the card holds a microchip with information about your account including your PIN number. When you buy something with your credit or debit card and enter your PIN in the machine, the PIN is checked against the card so that the shop knows it is your card.

a. When you next buy something, watch the process carefully.

b. Insert your card into the machine and read the display. The instructions will vary slightly between systems. In some cases, you are asked to confirm the amount you are paying, while in others the shop assistant will simply ask you to enter your PIN.

c. See what happens after you enter your PIN. The machine will often tell you not to remove your card. It will ask you to remove your card once the process is completed.

d. Watch the process each time you use a chip and PIN card.

3. Information from electronic displays

> **ICT Skill for Life standard**
>
> This task helps you to practise:
>
> ■ using ICT for a purpose
>
> ■ recognising interface features
>
> ■ recognising sources of information
>
> ■ getting simple information from an ICT-based source that matches requirements.

In many places, information is shown on an electronic display board. Railway stations, travel agents and airports all use electronic displays.

a. Visit your local railway station and use the electronic display boards to identify:

■ where the trains are going

■ what time the trains are leaving

■ from which platform the trains are leaving

■ whether the trains are on time or late.

b. Visit a local travel agent or bank, and observe the electronic display of the different rates of exchange. Identify:

■ how many dollars you can obtain for £1

■ how many euros you can obtain for £1.

c. Each time you see an electronic display, practise finding information.

> **Vocab**
>
> **Rows and columns** Rows are the horizontal lines of information in a table. Columns are the vertical lines of information in a table (see Figure 2.2).

d. Compare the different displays that you have seen. How many rows and columns of information were shown? What information was displayed and what symbols were used? As an example, Figure 2.2 shows a table of exchange rate information with three columns and five rows.

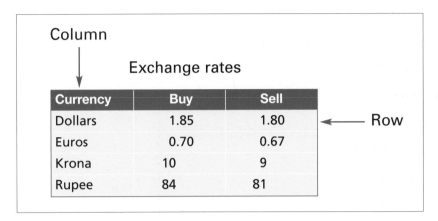

Figure 2.2 Information displays

Economic activity, including paid and unpaid work

1. Password

> **ICT Skill for Life standard**
>
> This task helps you to practise:
>
> ■ using ICT for a purpose
>
> ■ recognising and using interface features
>
> ■ entering and editing simple information
>
> ■ identifying and correcting simple errors
>
> ■ submitting information.

The majority of jobs now require you to use ICT. Organisations' computers are protected by passwords, and all employees have their own password and user name so they can use the computer. This is often called the 'user ID' or 'user identification'. Some systems remember the user ID so that you only need to enter a password.

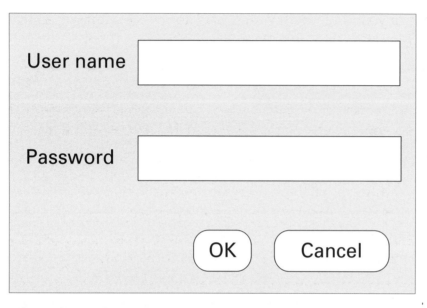

Figure 2.3 Passwords

Ask a friend, colleague or tutor to establish you as a user on a computer system with a password.

a. Enter your user name and then your password on the computer screen. You will notice that asterisks appear, such as ********, rather than your actual password. This is to prevent someone reading your password as you enter it. Figure 2.3 shows an example of a password window.

b. Click on the OK button and you should access the computer system.

c. If you make an error when typing your password, you will see a message appear such as 'Have you forgotten your password?' You will need to enter the password again.

2. Calculations

> **ICT Skill for Life standard**
>
> This task helps you to practise:
>
> - using ICT for a purpose
> - recognising and using interface features
> - entering and editing simple information
> - identifying and correcting simple errors
> - submitting information.

Ask a friend, colleague or your tutor to open the calculator on the computer as shown in Figure 2.4. The calculator is one of the Microsoft Windows® accessories.

Vocab

Accessories are extra applications that are included in a computer system.

Windows® is the brand name of a major software product. However, a 'window' is also a rectangular area of the display that can be adjusted in size to cover the whole display or it can be reduced to an icon. Computer applications and information are shown in windows.

Software is the instructions that make the equipment work. Software is installed on the computer and you do not need to enter it.

Figure 2.4 Calculator

a. You can operate the calculator by clicking on its buttons with the mouse. The mouse moves the mouse pointer. The symbols for different mathematical operations are as follows:

/   division

*   multiplication

–   subtraction

+   addition.

b. Use the calculator to work out some maths that is relevant to you.

For example, how many kilometres to the litre does your car do?

340 kilometres travelled using 15 litres of petrol.

340 divide by 15 = 22.67 kilometres per litre.

c. If you enter the wrong figure, click on the Backspace button on the calculator to delete.

d. If you need to remove your last entry, press the CE button. To clear the display, use the C button.

e. Carry on until you are confident that you can move the mouse pointer accurately.

f. Ask your friend, colleague or tutor to close the calculator.

Vocab

The **mouse** is a small piece of equipment that controls the mouse pointer on the screen.

The **mouse pointer** is a small pointer that appears on the screen display and is controlled by moving the mouse.

Clicking is the process of placing the mouse pointer over a control shown on the screen and pressing the mouse button to activate it.

Vocab

Backspace is a key on the keyboard or calculator that deletes a character to the left of the cursor.

When entering text using the keyboard, the **cursor** marks the place on screen where the new text will appear. It is often shown as a flashing bar.

Domestic and everyday life

1. Receive a text message

ICT Skill for Life standard

This task helps you to practise:

■ using ICT for a purpose

■ recognising and using interface features

■ recognising sources of information

■ receiving ICT-based communication.

Ask a friend, colleague or your tutor to send you a text message.

a. Inspect your mobile phone. They vary in appearance but try to identify the:

■ on/off switch

■ special keys that allow you to select or close a message

■ menu key – this is sometimes a different shape to the other keys and provides a variety of options

■ keyboard – you should notice that each key has several letters associated with it as well as a number

■ screen.

b. Switch on the phone.

c. Look at what is on the screen. You may notice a battery-shaped image; this is called an icon. The image indicates how much power is left in the battery. You may also notice a small image like a telegraph pole, and this icon indicates the strength of the signal. Figure 2.5 shows some examples of the icons.

Vocab

The **menu** gives a list of options from which you can choose.

An **icon** is a small picture on the display screen. Figure 2.5 shows some icons.

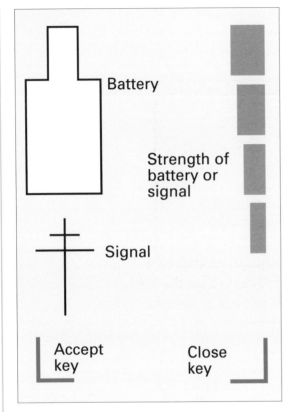

Battery

Strength of
battery or
signal

Signal

Accept
key

Close
key

Figure 2.5 Mobile phone icons

d. When a text message arrives, you will hear a tone or some music.

e. Use the accept key to read the text message.

f. Close the message and switch off the mobile phone.

2. Retrieve a voice mail message

> **ICT Skill for Life standard**
>
> This task helps you to practise:
>
> ■ using ICT for a purpose
>
> ■ recognising and using interface features
>
> ■ recognising sources of information
>
> ■ getting simple information from an ICT-based source that matches requirements
>
> ■ receiving ICT-based communication.

Ask a friend, colleague or your tutor to leave a voice mail message on your mobile phone.

a. Inspect your mobile phone.

b. Switch on the phone.

c. See what is on the screen.

d. Enter the number to access your voice mail.

e. Listen to your message and to what the system tells you. My voice mail says how many new messages I have received. It also explains what functions I can use by pressing different keys.

f. Close the voice mail box and switch off the mobile phone.

Leisure

1. Take a photograph with a digital camera

> **ICT Skill for Life standard**
>
> This task helps you to practise:
>
> - using ICT for a purpose
> - recognising and using interface features.

There are many different models of digital camera. This exercise assumes that the one you are using shows an image of the picture on a small screen.

a. Inspect the camera.

b. Can you see the following?

- an on/off switch
- a small screen
- controls – these are often in the form of icons or words
- a button to take a photograph, normally on the top right-hand side of the camera.

The different controls, screen and switch form the camera's interface.

c. Switch on the camera – the screen will light up, and the shutter protecting the lens will open.

d. Take a photograph.

e. Check the quality of the image on the screen. The picture will be shown for a few moments after you take it.

f. If you are not satisfied with the photograph, take another.

g. Switch the camera off when you have finished.

2. Using a digital radio

ICT Skill for Life standard

This task helps you to:

- recognise sources of information

- get simple information from an ICT-based source that matches requirements.

There are various types of digital radio. They all provide many choices of radio station to listen to.

a. Switch on your digital radio.

b. Search through the different channels and choose one that will provide news. I chose BBC Radio 4.

c. Listen to the news and then change the channel to one that offers music. I chose Saga.

d. Listen to the music and then change the channel to one that provides items about sport. I chose Talksport.

e. Continue until you are confident that you can find any channel.

f. Switch off the digital radio.

Education and training

1. Find out about courses at your local college

Many colleges now provide information about their courses on a website. Ask a friend, colleague or

ICT Skill for Life standard

This task helps you to practise:

- using ICT for a purpose

- recognising and using interface features

- recognising sources of information

- getting simple information from an ICT-based source that matches requirements.

tutor to find your local college's website and a page displaying course details. This page should be selected to match your interests, such as full- or part-time courses.

Vocab

A **page** in this context is part of a website that presents information to you.

a. Select a course that interests you.

b. Identify:
    - when the course will held
    - where the course will be held
    - the cost of the course
    - the content of the programme
    - if you can gain a qualification
    - advice about who should attend the course.

Vocab

A **hotspot** is an area in the website display that you can click on with the mouse and it takes you to another part of the website.

c. Click on any hotspots that interest you, and see what happens.

d. When you are finished ask your friend, colleague or tutor to close the internet system.

2. Find out about your local school

ICT Skills for Life standard

This task helps you to practise:

- using ICT for a purpose
- recognising and using interface features
- recognising sources of information
- getting simple information from an ICT-based source that matches requirements.

Many primary and secondary schools now have websites that give information about them. Ask a friend, colleague or tutor to find your local school website and to position you on the home page.

> ## Vocab
> A **home page** is the first page of a website.

a. Read the information provided and, using the mouse pointer, select a link that interests you.

b. Try to find a picture of the school or its address and telephone number.

> ## Vocab
> A **link** is a connection between one part of a website and another.

c. Look for the school's admissions policy.

d. Explore the website until you are satisfied that you know some basic information about the school.

e. When you are finished ask your friend, colleague or tutor to close the internet system.

Safe practices

It is always important to be safe when using equipment. It is essential to follow the instructions about safety matters. Some key points are:

1. Adjust the chair correctly so you are comfortable when using a computer.

2. Position the computer monitor to minimise reflections and glare.

3. Ensure that everything is tidy so that people do not trip over the computer cables.

> ## Vocab
> The **monitor** is a device that presents the computer's information. It resembles a television.

4. Have regular breaks away from the computer.

Ask for help from your tutor if you feel that something is wrong or if you need to adjust your seat or the computer monitor.

Summary

Here are some useful tasks for you to do:

■ Identify different forms of ICT.

■ Try to identify the purpose of different pieces of equipment.

■ Practise entering your user name and password on a computer.

■ Practise entering your PIN for your credit or debit card.

■ Practise entering and submitting simple information on an interface display.

■ Practise receiving text and voice messages on your mobile phone.

■ Practise using electronic sources of information.

■ Always follow the safety instructions.

■ Never show or tell anyone your password.

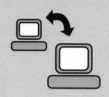
Objectives

This chapter will help you to:

- recognise and use interface features
- use hardware
- use software applications
- follow recommended safe practices
- keep access information secure.

Qualifications

This chapter will help you if you are studying for a qualification awarded by:

- OCR
- City and Guilds
- Edexcel.

Assessment

Each qualification is assessed through assignments. These are practical tasks that relate to your use of ICT. The details of the assessment vary between the awarding bodies so ask your tutor for details.

Interface features

In your home you may find:

- an alarm clock
- an oven

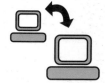

- a microwave
- a telephone
- a digital or other radio
- a mobile phone
- a video recorder
- a television
- a computer
- a digital camera.

These devices all have electronic displays. The displays essentially serve the same purpose and have many things in common – they help you to communicate with or to instruct the device. The displays offer you information about the devices' settings so that you know when you have successfully communicated your needs. This is called an 'interface'.

You may want to select a radio channel, set a video recorder to record a programme, switch on the microwave for five minutes or set an alarm clock. The skill and knowledge needed to interact with these devices through the interface are very similar to the skill and knowledge you need when using a computer. You will be able to transfer these skills to using a computer.

Icons

Most interfaces use small pictures to make the controls easier to understand. These pictures are called 'icons'. Figures 3.1 and 3.2 illustrate two interfaces and some icons. The Enter button in Figure 3.1 is shown with the word 'Enter' and a bent arrow, while in Figure 3.2 it is a circular green button with a symbol in the middle. Both controls serve similar purposes. When you press Enter ⬅ , you confirm that you

Vocab

Enter is a term with several meanings. In this case, it is the name of a button or a key on a keyboard. When you press 'Enter' ⬅ on the keyboard, you confirm that you have finished an action.

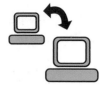

have finished an action. For example, with a burglar alarm, pressing Enter submits confirmation of the alarm setting.

Figure 3.1 Control box

Figure 3.2 Controls

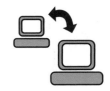

The finger and the pointer

To use the devices shown in Figures 3.1 and 3.2, you need to press buttons with your finger. When you press a button, you are inputting information. On a computer, you carry out similar actions with the keyboard or a mouse and mouse pointer. These devices are generally called input devices, while the screen is known as an output device.

Vocab

Input devices are pieces of equipment that let you enter information into ICT, for example a keyboard or a mouse.

Output devices are pieces of equipment that show the results of a task, for example a monitor or a printer.

Option buttons

Both the devices illustrated in Figures 3.1 and 3.2 offer extra options. In Figure 3.2 there is a button with an icon showing a question mark. This is the help button. In Figure 3.1, the help button is labelled 'Help'. There are other options such as quit (see Figure 3.1) and cancel (shown by a button with the letter 'C' in Figure 3.2).

Menus

In this context, a menu is a list of options displayed on a screen. Figure 3.3 shows a computer display. This is a Microsoft Windows Professional XP® desktop showing the 'Start' menu. Notice that almost all items have an icon as well as a name. Some items have an arrow alongside them, for example 'Connect To'. This shows that additional options will appear when you select the item.

Vocab

The main computer display is called the **desktop**. Microsoft Windows® opens to show the desktop.

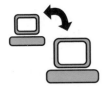

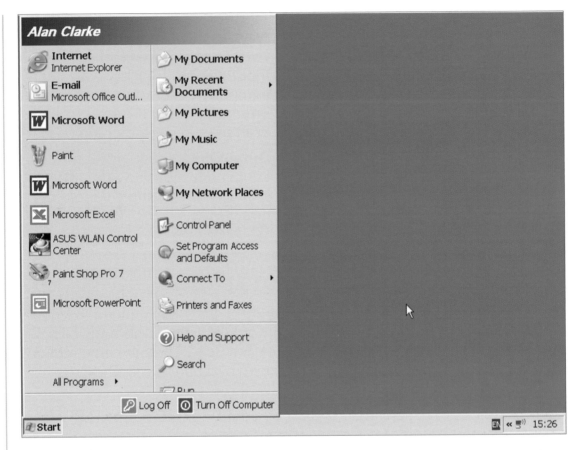

Figure 3.3 'Start' menu

Applications

The two most widely used computer applications are probably word processing and spreadsheets. A word processor allows you to produce written documents such as letters. A spreadsheet helps you to use numbers.

Figure 3.4 shows the opening display of Microsoft Word® 2003. You will notice a bar called a cursor. The cursor flashes on the computer. When you type in text from the keyboard, it will appear at the cursor. Microsoft Word® provides you with many options and functions that are available from the menu, toolbar and task pane areas. The work area where the text appears can be moved both right and left and up and down. This is called 'scrolling'. It is controlled by the scroll bars.

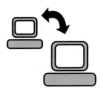

Menu

Toolbar

Cursor

Task pane

Work area

Scroll bars

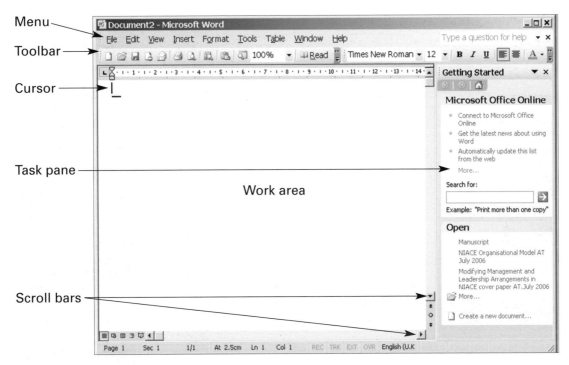

Figure 3.4 Microsoft Word® 2003

Figure 3.5 shows the opening display of Microsoft Excel® 2003. The work area is divided up into rows and columns to form a grid of cells. You can enter numbers and words from the keyboard in the active cell. The active cell is shown by a black border. You can change the active cell by moving the mouse pointer to another cell and clicking your mouse. Microsoft Excel® provides you with many options and functions that are available from the menu, toolbar and task pane areas. The work area moves both right and left and up and down.

Vocab

A **cell** is the area formed when spreadsheet rows and columns intersect.

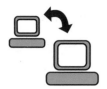

Menu

Toolbar

Column

Active cell

Task pane

Row

Scroll bars

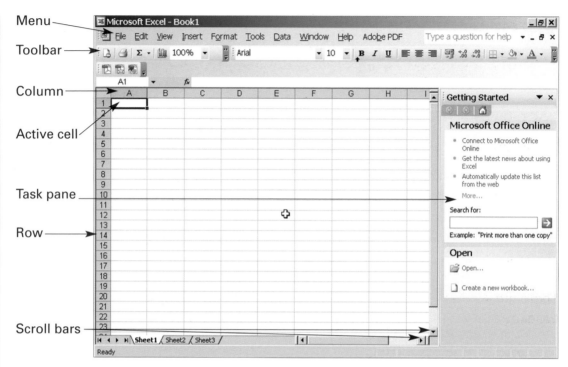

Figure 3.5 Microsoft Excel® 2003

Practical tasks

This section contains a variety of tasks. They allow you to practise many of the skills required in Entry Level 2 'Using ICT systems'. You can do the tasks in any order, and it is not necessary to complete them all. The tasks also provide opportunities to find and exchange information and to develop and present information. They are therefore relevant to the standards covered in Chapters 4 and 5 as well.

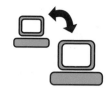

Citizen and community

1. Find train times for a journey you are planning

ICT Skill for Life standard

This task helps you to practise:

- using hardware and software applications

- recognising and using interface features.

Vocab

Interface features are the controls that appear on the display, for example icons and buttons.

There are several websites that provide details of train times. Ask a friend, colleague or your tutor to find one for you. For example:

www.thetrainline.com

www.nationalrail.co.uk

www.tfl.gov.uk

a. Enter details of your journey.

You will notice that the website page asks you to enter information about the journey you are planning to take. The exact words will depend on the particular site but you are likely to be asked for:

Vocab

Enter has more than one meaning in ICT. In this case, it means typing in information using the keyboard.

A **site** is a website on the World Wide Web.

- the date and time of your outbound journey

- the date and time of your return journey.

You may need to enter the data in the 'day/month/year' format. For example, 3 August 2006 would be shown as 03/08/06. An example will often be shown to guide you.

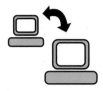

The time is in the form of a 24-hour clock. For example, 3.30pm is shown as 15:30. In some cases you will have to choose the time of your journey from a drop-down list.

Check that the information you have entered is correct. If you have made an error, just enter the information again.

When you have entered the time, click on a button called **Get Times** if you are using www.thetrainline. com, **Get Train Times** if you are using www.nationalrail.co.uk, or the new journey button if you are using www.tfl.gov.uk. Figure 3.6 shows a typical display.

Vocab

A **button** is an area of the display that you can click with the mouse. It will then start an action.

b. You will be presented with a list of trains that are available for the time and date you have chosen.

c. You can often get more details about each train by clicking on a button such as 'More Information'. There will also be options to see details of

Figure 3.6 Train times

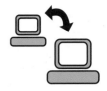

earlier and later trains. Explore the options. You can go back a step by clicking on the Back button on the top of the screen. There is also a 'Forward' button. Try them both. They are sometimes shown as arrows enclosed in circles: 'Back' has a left-pointing arrow and 'Forward' a right-pointing arrow.

Vocab

The **Back button** is an option in the top left-hand corner of Microsoft Internet Explorer® that allows you to retrace your steps between links.

d. There are other options you can explore by using the Back and Forward buttons. Figure 3.10 (see page 38) shows the Back button in the top left-hand corner.

e. When you are confident that you understand what the website offers, print the page showing the train times. You will probably hear the printer start to print.

f. Close down the application and switch off the system.

2. Write a short note

ICT Skill for Life standard

This task helps you to practise:

■ using hardware and software applications

■ recognising and using interface features.

There are occasions when you will need to write a brief note to a friend, school teacher, postman or partner. Switch on a computer with Microsoft Windows® installed. Open Microsoft Word® (see Figure 3.4) and switch on the printer. My example in Figure 3.7 is based on a note to a neighbour saying that I am going to be away for the weekend.

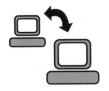

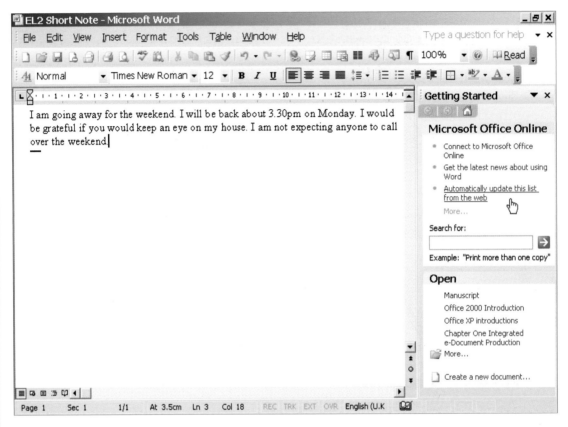

Figure 3.7 Short note

a. Look at the display. It should look like Figure 3.4 (see page 27). Try to identify the menu, toolbar, task pane, scroll bars and cursor.

b. Type your text into Microsoft Word® using the keyboard. If you are new to keyboards, it will require practice to become familiar with the layout. Notice that when you type, the letters appear at the cursor. When you fill a line, the text will automatically start a new line. This is called 'wrap around'.

c. If you make a mistake, press the 'Backspace' key. This is sometimes shown by a left-pointing arrow on the key. It will delete the letter to the left. You can then enter the letter again.

d. When you are confident that you have correctly entered your note, print it out if your computer is linked to a printer. That is, click on the File menu, Print option and OK button. You will probably hear the printer start to print.

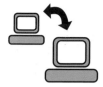

e. Click on the arrow buttons on the bottom and right end of the scroll bars and see what happens. The page will move until your note disappears.

f. Explore by moving the page with the arrow buttons.

g. Close down the application and switch off the system.

Economic activity, including paid and unpaid work

1. Make a list

> **ICT Skill for Life standard**
>
> This task helps you to practise:
>
> ■ using hardware and software applications
>
> ■ recognising and using interface features.

For many work tasks, you need to create lists. These may be lists of:

■ things you need to do

■ equipment you need

■ names of people who are attending a meeting.

Switch on a computer with Microsoft Windows® installed and open Microsoft Excel® (see Figure 3.5, page 28). My example in Figure 3.8 is based on a list of stationery items I need. You are going to create a list to meet your needs.

a. Look around the display. It should resemble Figure 3.5 (see page 28). Try to identify the menu, toolbar, task pane, scroll bars, rows and columns, and active cell.

b. Enter your text into Microsoft Excel® using the keyboard. It does not matter how long this takes. If you are new to keyboards, it will require practice to become familiar with the layout. Notice that the letters you type appear in the active cell. When you want to enter a new item, you need to put the

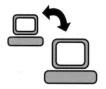

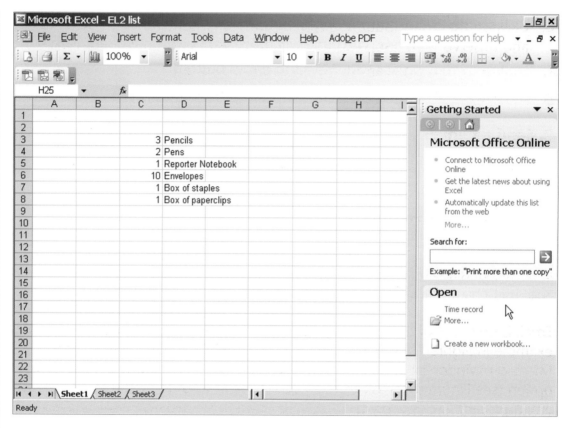

Figure 3.8 List

mouse pointer in the cell below and click the mouse button.

c. If you make a mistake, press the 'Backspace' or 'Delete' keys. This will delete the contents of the cell. You can then enter the word again.

d. When you are confident that you have correctly entered your list, print it out if your computer is linked to a printer. You need to click on the File menu, Print option and OK button. You will probably hear the printer start to print.

Vocab

A mouse normally has two **mouse buttons**. You press the left button to confirm an action. The right button will open up new menus of options in some cases.

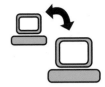

e. Click on the arrow buttons on the bottom and right end of the scroll bars and observe what happens. The page will move until your list disappears.

f. Explore by using the arrow keys to move the page.

g. Close down the application and switch off the system.

2. Send an email

> **ICT Skill for Life standard**
>
> This task helps you to practise:
>
> ■ using hardware and software applications
>
> ■ recognising and using interface features.

Email is now one of the main ways in which people communicate at work. My example in Figure 3.9 is based on a meeting. Switch on a computer with Microsoft Windows® installed, open Microsoft Outlook® and select the Email option (see Figure 3.9). Ask a friend, colleague or tutor to provide you with an email address or use one you know. Create an email message appropriate to your needs to send to this email address.

a. Try to find the areas on the message called 'To' and 'Subject'.

b. To send an email message you need to:

■ enter an email address in the 'To' box such as alan@skillforlife.co.uk

■ enter a subject; this is the title of the message

■ enter your message

■ click on the Send button.

c. Click in the 'To' box and the text you type on the keyboard will appear in it.

d. If you make a mistake, press the 'Backspace' key. This is sometimes shown by a left-pointing arrow on the key. It will delete letters to the left. After you have deleted the letters, type them in again correctly.

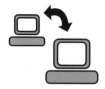

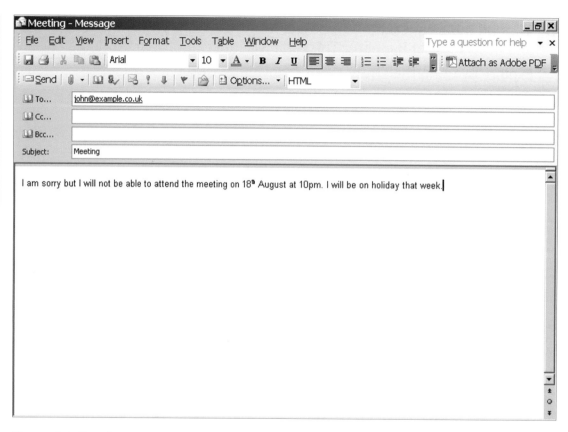

Figure 3.9 Email

e. Click in the 'Subject' box and the text you type on the keyboard will appear in it.

f. Click in the message area and enter your message.

g. Check the address, subject and message again. To correct errors, click at the end of the word and delete using 'Backspace', and then enter the correct text.

h. When you are ready, click on the Send button.

i. Close down the email application and switch off the computer.

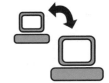

Domestic and everyday life

1. Shop online

Online shopping is one of the most popular uses of the internet. Ask a friend, colleague or your tutor to find a website that sells products you are interested in. Some sites that you might choose include:

- books – www.amazon.co.uk

- computers – www.pcworld.co.uk

- groceries – www.tesco.com

- stationery – www.staples.co.uk

- holidays – www.thomson.co.uk

In order to view a website, you need an application called a 'browser'. Figure 3.10 shows the browser Microsoft Internet Explorer® 6.0. A website called 'Money Matters to me' is shown in the browser.

Web pages can be far longer than the page in a book. However, the browser only lets you see part of the page. It acts like a window on a long roll of paper. Figure 3.11 illustrates the length of a web page. You can move up and down or left or right using the scroll bar.

Vocab

Web pages are sections of a website where information is displayed.

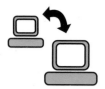

Figure 3.10 Microsoft Internet Explorer®

a. Enter the address of the website into a browser and press the 'Return' key to open the site.

b. Explore the web page and try to identify who owns the site. It may be shown by a button option called 'About Us'. Click on the button and more information will be shown.

c. Words that are underlined are called 'hyperlinks', sometimes shortened to 'links'. When you click on them, you will move to another part of the website. Click on some hyperlinks to see what happens.

d. When you place your mouse pointer over a link, the pointer changes shape to form a hand. This shows you that it is a link. Move the pointer around the web page and try to find more links. Pictures sometimes act as links.

e. A shopping site will often have lists of products. Select what interests you and click on the link. You will move to another part of the website.

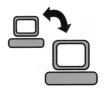

f. If you want to go back to the previous page, click on the Back button on the menu.

g. If you click on the arrow buttons on the bottom and right end of the scroll bars, the page will move right and left or up and down. Try this to see what happens.

h. Explore the website until you are confident that you can find your way around it.

i. If you want to buy any of the products, ask for help from your friend, colleague or tutor.

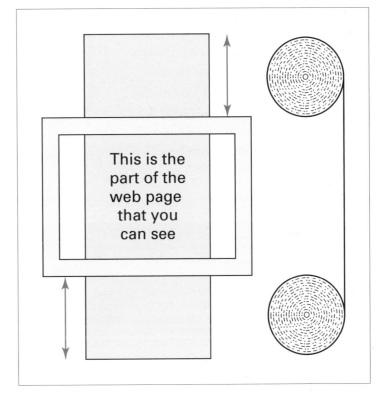

This is the part of the web page that you can see

Figure 3.11 Web page

j. Close the website and switch off the computer.

2. Create a simple design

ICT Skill for Life standard

This task helps you to practise:

- using hardware and software applications
- recognising and using interface features.

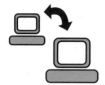

There are times when you may need to draw a diagram to help you with DIY, the layout of furniture, garden design or decorating your home. There are many different computer applications to help you create an image. They are normally called 'graphics applications'. Microsoft Windows® includes a graphics application called Paint®. This is shown in Figure 3.12.

Vocab

Graphic means a picture, drawing or shape.

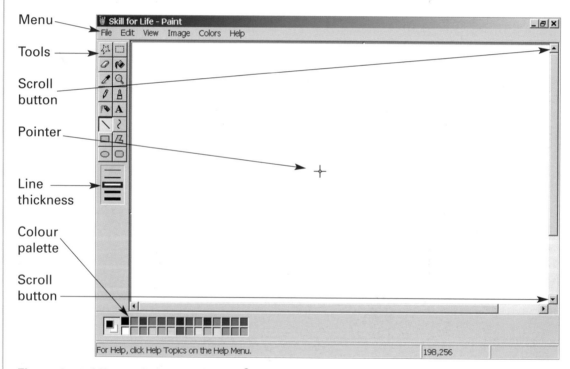

Figure 3.12 Microsoft Windows Paint®

a. Switch on the computer and open Microsoft Windows Paint® by clicking on the Start button, highlighting the All Programs and Accessories options and clicking on Paint.

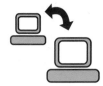

b. Explore the application interface and try to find the:

- menu
- tools
- pointer
- colour palette
- scroll bars.

c. The tools help you to draw different shapes, for example a straight line, rectangle and a circle. Practise making different drawings using the tools.

d. You can change the colour of your drawing by clicking on the colours in the palette.

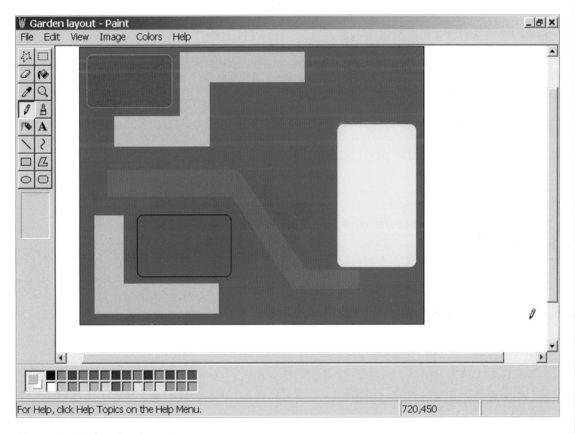

Figure 3.13 Garden layout

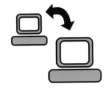

e. If you place the mouse pointer over each tool, you will see that a label appears giving you the name of the tool. One of the tools is called 'Select'. You can drag different parts of a drawing around using this tool. Try to move an object using the tool.

f. Try to draw a diagram of something relevant to you. Figure 3.13 shows a garden layout.

g. Continue to use Microsoft Windows Paint® until you are able to draw something that meets your needs.

h. Close the application and switch off the computer.

Leisure

1. Take a photograph with a digital camera

There are many types of digital camera but they will usually have the following features:

- an on/off switch
- a screen to show the photograph you are taking
- a zoom
- a memory card to store your pictures
- a menu
- control buttons
- a photograph button
- a video button.

For such a small device, there are a lot of controls on a digital camera.

a. Inspect the camera. Can you see the following?

- an on/off switch
- a small screen

> **ICT Skill for Life standard**
>
> This task helps you to practise:
>
> - using hardware
> - recognising and using interface features.

> **Vocab**
>
> A **memory card** is a small portable card on which information can be stored, for example digital photographs. It fits inside the camera.

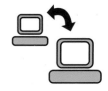

- controls – they are often shown as icons
- a button to take a photograph (normally on the top right-hand side of the camera).

b. Switch on the camera – the screen will light up and the shutter protecting the lens will open.

c. Take several photographs of things that interest you.

d. Check the quality of each image by finding the replay control or switch. This is sometimes shown by a picture of an arrow. The control will allow you to see each image in turn.

e. Use the zoom control to take photographs of things that interest you. Again, check the quality.

f. Use the menu control to delete any poor photographs.

g. Practise with the camera until you are confident.

h. Switch the camera off.

2. Play a game

There are many different computer games. Microsoft Windows® has several built in. You can find the games by clicking on the Start button, highlighting the All Programs and then the Games options to reveal a list.

> **ICT Skill for Life standard**
>
> This task helps you to practise:
>
> - using hardware and software applications
> - recognising and using interface features.

Switch on a computer with Microsoft Windows® installed and find the games (see Figure 3.14). Select one that interests you (I chose Solitaire). The rules for the game are available by clicking on the Help button and the Contents option. They are shown in Figure 3.15.

a. Look around the display and identify the Help menu.

b. Explore Help – you can return to the game by clicking on the X button in the top right-hand corner. This closes the 'Help' window.

c. Play the game. The opening display is shown in Figure 3.16. You move cards by putting the mouse pointer on them, clicking and holding down

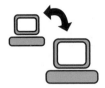

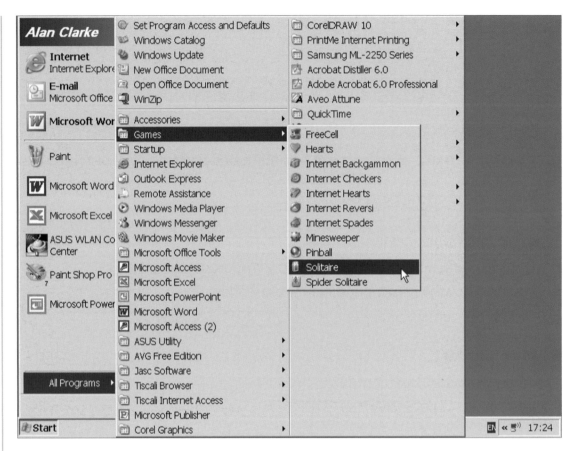

Figure 3.14 Microsoft Windows® games

the mouse button, dragging the card to a new location, and releasing the button. This is called 'drag and drop'. You turn the pack over by clicking on it.

d. If you make a mistake, the card will return to where you dragged it from.

e. Play the game until you are confident that you are doing your best. Close the game and switch the computer off.

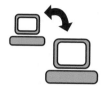

Figure 3.15 Solitaire 'Help'

Extra practice

Using the mouse to drag and drop can be a difficult skill to learn. Switch on the computer. The Microsoft Windows® desktop will appear. You will see a number of icons. These can be moved using drag and drop. To do this, put the mouse pointer on them, click once and hold down the mouse button, and then move the pointer. The image will move with you. When you release the button, the image stays in its new position.

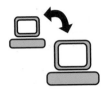

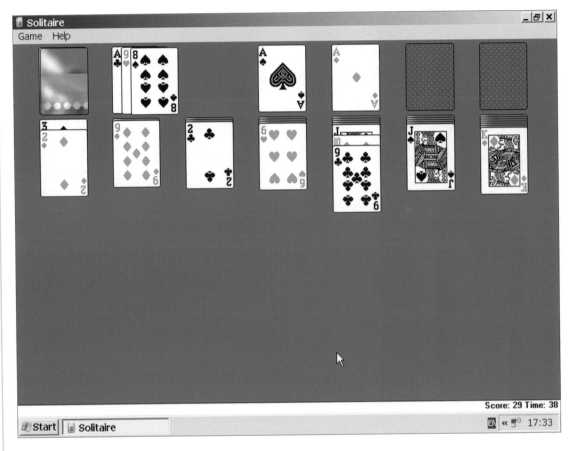

Figure 3.16 Solitaire

a. Move the icons to form a pattern of your choice. Figure 3.17 shows my pattern.

b. Return the images to their original positions.

c. Ask a friend, your tutor or another learner for help if you get stuck.

d. Switch off the computer when you have finished.

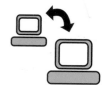

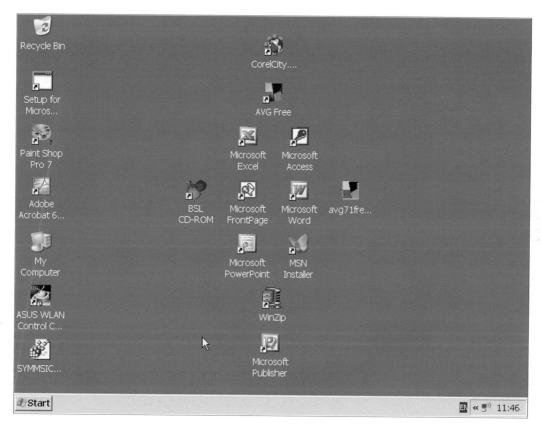

Figure 3.17 Microsoft Windows® desktop pattern

Education and training

1. Using 'Help and Support'

Switch on a computer that has
Microsoft Windows® installed.
Microsoft Windows® is an operating
system that controls the way the
computer works. All operating
systems offer help to users.

> **ICT Skill for Life standard**
>
> This task helps you to practise:
>
> ■ using hardware and software
>   applications
>
> ■ recognising and using interface
>   features.

a. Click on the <u>S</u>tart button and you will see a menu appear. Figure 3.3 (see
page 26) shows the menu for the Microsoft Windows Professional XP®
operating system.

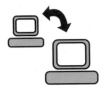

b. On this menu is an option called 'Help and Support'. In other operating systems, the name may vary but it will normally include the word 'Help'. Click on this option to open the 'Help' window. Figure 3.18 shows the 'Help and Support' window in the Microsoft Windows Professional XP® system.

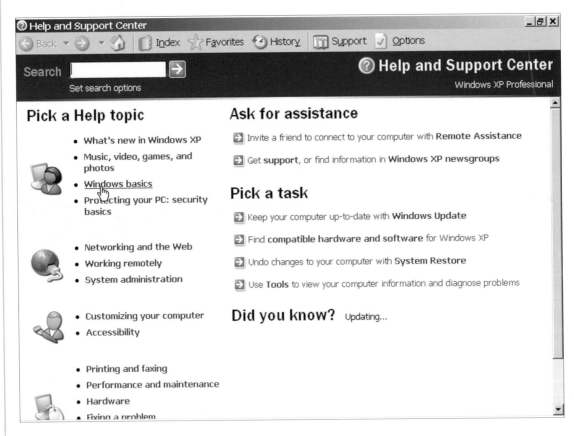

Figure 3.18 Help and Support

c. Explore the different options. When you place your mouse pointer over a topic, it will become underlined. This indicates a link with more information. Click again to access the information. Microsoft Windows® Help gives assistance by providing a short tutorial about the chosen subject. In Microsoft Windows XP® Help, you will notice information about:

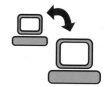

- Microsoft Windows® basics: that is, how to use the Windows® operating system

- protecting your PC: security basics

- accessibility: that is, help if you are a user with disabilities

- hardware.

d. Explore a topic that is relevant to you – you can return to a previous web page by using the Back button on the top of the display.

> ## Vocab
>
> **PC** is the abbreviation for Personal Computer.
>
> **Accessibility** is about making the computer system more suitable for people to use.

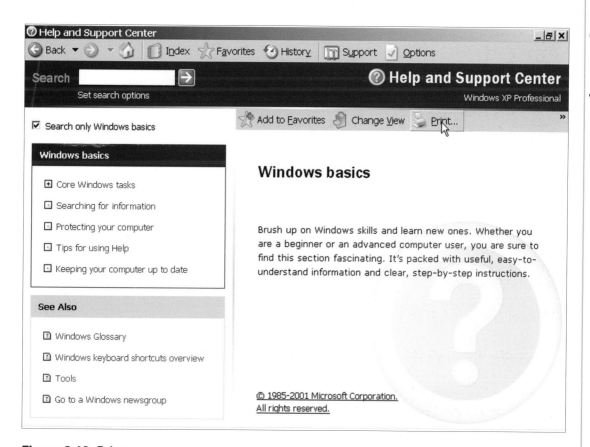

Figure 3.19 Print

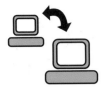

e. You can print the information that interests you if your computer is connected to a printer (see Figure 3.19).

f. Continue to explore the different options using the Back and Forward buttons and links until you have learned about your selected topics.

g. Close the Help system and switch the computer off when you have finished.

2. Exploring a website

The World Wide Web has been described as an enormous library of information. It is probably one of the best resources to help you learn. Ask a friend, colleague or your tutor to find a website that interests you. Some sites that you might choose include:

> **ICT Skill for Life standard**
>
> This task helps you to practise:
>
> ■ using hardware and software applications
>
> ■ recognising and using interface features.

- ■ The Domesday Book: www.domesdaybook.co.uk
- ■ The British Museum: www.thebritishmuseum.ac.uk
- ■ The British Library: www.bl.uk
- ■ The Imperial War Museum: www.iwm.org.uk

In order to view a website, you need an application called a 'browser' such as Microsoft Internet Explorer® 6.0 (see Figure 3.10, page 38).

Web pages can be far longer than the page in a book. However, the browser only allows you to see part of the page. It acts like a window on a long roll of paper (see Figure 3.11, page 39). You can move up and down using the scroll bar or left or right.

a. Enter the address of the website into the browser.

b. Explore the web page and find out who controls the site. This may be shown by an option called 'About Us'. Click on the option and more information will be revealed.

c. Words that are underlined are called 'hyperlinks', sometimes shortened to 'links'. When you click on them, you move to another part of the website.

d. When you place your mouse pointer over a link, it changes shape to form a hand. This shows you that it is a link. Move the pointer around the web page and try to find more links. Pictures can sometimes act as links.

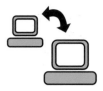

e. A website will often have lists of options. Select what interests you and click on the link. You will move to another part of the website.

f. If you want to return to a previous page, then click on the Back button on the menu.

g. If you click on the arrow buttons on the bottom and right end of the scroll bars, the page will move right and left or up and down. Try them and see what happens.

h. Explore the website until you are confident that you can find your way around it.

i. If you find information that you would like to copy, select the File menu, Print option and click on the OK button (assuming your computer is connected to a printer). You may hear the printer start and a copy of the web page will appear. There may be several sheets of paper since a web page is often longer than a book page.

j. Close the browser and switch off the computer.

Safe practices

Here are some actions that will keep you healthy and safe when using a computer:

1. Adjust the chair so that it is comfortable, or ask for help to do so. You should be able to see the computer display and reach the controls without any need to stretch or twist your body. Your feet should be flat on the ground and your eyes level with the top quarter of the display.

2. Adjust the computer display screen so that there are no reflections from the room lights or from the sun.

3. Check that there are no cables around the computer to trip over. Never have drinks or other liquids near a computer. Electricity and drinks do not mix. Look around the area to make sure everything is safe.

4. It is important to take regular breaks away from computers.

5. A few moments of effort will ensure that you are comfortable. Ask for help from your tutor if you feel something is wrong or if you are unable to carry out any of the tasks.

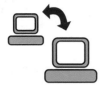

Security

You must keep your user identification and password private. You should not share the information with anyone. Try to avoid writing down the details and memorise them instead. Treat your password as you would treat your credit card information – it is just as important.

The computer identifies users by their user identification and password. If someone knows your password, they can log on to the computer system. The computer system will then assume the user is you. Everything the user does will be identified as undertaken by you. Do not allow anyone to watch you entering your password.

Summary

Here are some useful tasks for you to do:

- Explore all the equipment and applications that you come into contact with such as digital cameras and computers. Identify similarities and differences between them.

- Compare the different interface controls of all forms of ICT. For example, look at a mobile telephone and a computer. Identify the similarities and differences between them.

- Compare how different applications work. For example, look at text messages and emails. Identify the similarities and differences between them.

- Practise using the keyboard and mouse.

- Take care of yourself – health and safety are vital. It should always be your first priority.

- Never show or tell anyone your password.

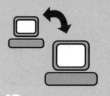
Objectives

This chapter will help you to:

- recognise and use appropriate sources of ICT and other forms of information
- find information from an ICT-based source using appropriate facilities
- use ICT to communicate.

Qualifications

This chapter will help you if you are studying for a qualification awarded by:

- OCR
- City and Guilds
- Edexcel.

Applications

Two computer applications that are important for finding and exchanging information are:

- browsers
- email systems.

A browser is an application that allows you to read web pages and to move around websites. There is a variety of applications such as Microsoft Internet

> ### Vocab
>
> **Using appropriate sources of ICT** means that you need to choose the correct ICT equipment and approach to achieve what you want, for example choosing the best way to send a message.
>
> **Using appropriate facilities** means that you need to choose the most suitable way to achieve what you want, for example choosing the best way to find the local weather forecast.

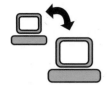

Explorer®, Mozilla Firefox®, Netscape® and Opera®. Some are designed to help visually impaired users by reading the text out loud. Browsealoud® is an example of a speaking browser. Figure 4.1 shows Microsoft Internet Explorer®, which is probably the most widely used browser in the world at the moment.

Each website has a unique address. When this is entered into the browser it will find the site. The address is sometimes called a URL meaning Universal Resource Locator. Some examples of addresses are:

http://www.bbc.co.uk

http://www.amazon.com

http://www.ageconcern.org.uk

http://www.pm.gov.uk

A website address is similar to a postal address:

'http' means hypertext transfer protocol, which is the technical term for how you move around websites

'www' means World Wide Web – the network of millions of websites around the world

'bbc', 'amazon', 'ageconcern' or 'pm' – these are the domain names or the name of who owns the site

'co' or 'com' means it is a commercial website

'org' means it is a site owned by a charity

'gov' means it is a government site

'ac' – means an academic (educational) site.

> ## Vocab
>
> A **domain** is part of a website address. It is often the name of the website owner or provider.

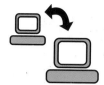

Menu

Address bar

Back button

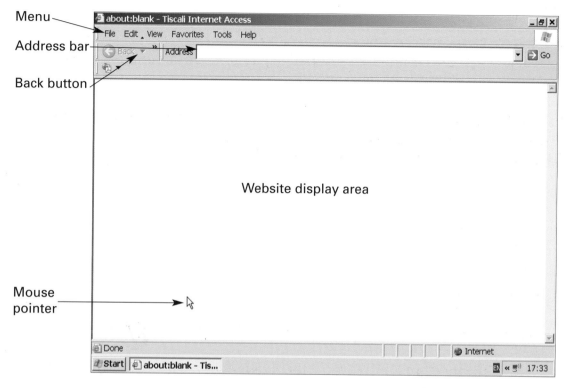

Website display area

Mouse pointer

Figure 4.1 Microsoft Internet Explorer®

Email systems let you receive and send messages. There are many different email applications available. Microsoft Outlook® is a sophisticated product (see Figure 4.2). It has a variety of features to organise your communications. Everyone using email needs their own email address. This is in the form:

name@domain.type of organisation.country

'name' – usually refers to the individual or organisation

'domain' – the organisation providing the email service or a company

'type of organisation' – there is a variety of codes such as 'co' (company), 'ac' (education) and 'net' (network)

'country' – usually shown as the country letters such as UK for United Kingdom.

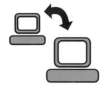

For example:

john@kingston.co.uk

hilary.jones@british.bananas.org.uk

The name and domain can be single or multiple words.

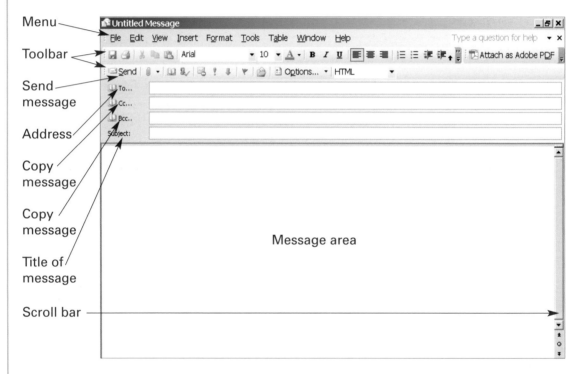

Menu
Toolbar
Send message
Address
Copy message
Copy message
Title of message
Scroll bar

Message area

Figure 4.2 Microsoft Outlook® email

Practical tasks

This section contains a variety of tasks. They allow you to practise many of the skills required in Entry Level 2 'Finding and exchanging information'. You can do the tasks in any order, and it is not necessary to complete them all. The tasks also provide opportunities to use ICT systems and to develop and present information. They are therefore relevant to the standards covered in Chapters 3 and 5 as well.

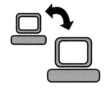

Citizen and community

1. Send a mobile phone text message

> **ICT Skill for Life standard**
>
> This task helps you to practise:
>
> - recognising and using appropriate sources of ICT
> - using ICT to communicate.

Mobile phone text messages are used by many people to keep in touch with their friends, family and colleagues. The official name is 'SMS' or 'Short Message Service', but they are better known as 'text messages' or just 'texts'. You can only send short messages of around 140–60 characters. Each letter is a character, so using abbreviations is important.

a. Inspect your mobile phone. Phones vary in appearance but just try to identify the main controls.

b. Switch on the phone.

c. Look at what is on the screen. You may notice battery- and telegraph-pole-shaped images (icons). These indicate battery life and the strength of the signal.

d. Many television and radio programmes encourage viewers and listeners to send comments by text message. Select a programme that interests you and send the programme makers a text message. For example:

U should ask 4 more help

e. To send a message, you need to find the menu key and then the message and text options. Write a text message to the programme.

f. Switch off your mobile phone.

Alternatively, in Chapter 2 you received a text message (see Task 1, page 15). Send a reply. Try to have a conversation by using text messages with your friend.

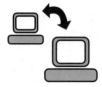

2. News

> **ICT Skill for Life standard**
>
> This task helps you to practise:
>
> ■ recognising and using appropriate sources of ICT
>
> ■ finding information from an ICT-based source using appropriate facilities.

There are lots of ways to find out the latest news through the use of technology. One of the first ways was to look at Teletext, which you are now going to do.

a. Switch on your television.

b. Use the remote control to select the Teletext service.

c. Read the display and identify a news item. The item may be accessed by pressing a colour-coded key on the remote control or by entering a 'page' number, such as 101.

d. Try to identify different ways of accessing the news stories. For example, use the Top Story or Next News buttons, or enter 103.

e. Find and read the top three news items.

f. Find other items of information that interest you, for example weather, sport, lottery results or what's on at the local cinema.

g. When you are confident that you can find information, close the Teletext display.

h. Switch off your television.

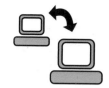

Economic activity, including paid and unpaid work

1. Plan a journey

> **ICT Skill for Life standard**
>
> This task helps you to practise:
>
> ■ recognising and using appropriate sources of ICT
>
> ■ finding information from an ICT-based source using appropriate facilities.

There are many websites that will help you to plan a journey. Ask a friend, colleague or your tutor to provide you with the address of one. For example:

Google Maps: http://maps.google.co.uk (see Figure 4.3)

The AA: www.theaa.com/travelwatch/planner_main.jsp

Multimap: www.multimap.com/map/aproute.cgi?input_rt=aproute_pan

a. Enter the address of the journey-planning website into the browser.

b. Carefully read the instructions on the web page. Sites will differ, but normally you need to enter:

    i. details of the place where your journey will start

    ii. details of the place where your journey will end.

c. You need to be precise, using postcodes, street names and the town name.

d. You will normally need to click on a button labelled 'Route' or something similar.

e. The route will then be shown. For example:

    1. 0.1 miles   Turn left on to Central Avenue

    2. 0.3 miles   Continue towards Kings Road

    3. 1.3 miles   Turn right at Lion Street

f. In some cases a map will also be displayed or there will be an option to show a map. Find the option and click on it.

g. Print the directions and the map – ideally using a colour printer.

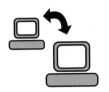

Figure 4.3 Google Maps

h. Explore the other options on the website such as shortest route or quickest route.

i. Change the options and repeat the process to compare the different routes.

j. Close the browser and computer system.

2. Send an email about work

Email is an important communication method at work. Many employees will receive and send dozens of messages each day. Email is also widely used in education, in our personal lives and in community activities.

> **ICT Skill for Life standard**
>
> This task helps you to practise:
>
> ■ using ICT to communicate.

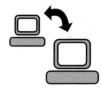

a. Open an email system, such as Microsoft Outlook®.

b. Explore the display as shown in Figure 4.2 (page 56) and try to identify:

    i. the address line

    ii. the subject line

    iii. the message area

    iv. the send button.

c. Write a message in connection with your work or another subject relevant to your. For example:

> Hi Jean
>
> We have a meeting next Tuesday at 11a.m. I would be grateful if you could send me directions to your office, or a map.
>
> Best wishes
>
> Alan

d. To send the message, you need to enter the recipient's email address in the line starting with 'To'. Then write the subject of the message in the line starting 'Subject'.

e. Once you have typed in your message, the address and the subject, send it by clicking on the Send button.

f. Close the email application and switch off the computer when you have finished.

If you are studying with a group of people, it can be useful to send each other messages so that you can see what a message looks like when it is received.

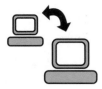

Domestic and everyday life

1. Find out about healthy lifestyles

> **ICT Skill for Life standard**
>
> This task helps you to practise:
>
> ■ recognising and using appropriate sources of ICT
>
> ■ finding information from an ICT-based source using appropriate facilities.

There is a variety of websites that will help you live in a healthy way. Ask a friend, colleague or your tutor to provide you with the address of one that enables you to calculate how many calories you will use when exercising in different ways. For example:

NHS Direct: www.nhsdirect.nhs.uk/interactiveTools/ExerciseCalorieCounter.aspx#ResultsSection

Calorie Control Council: www.caloriecontrol.org/exercalc.html

The Fitness Jumpsite: www.primusweb.com/fitnesspartner/jumpsite/calculat.htm

a. Enter the address of the exercise website into the browser.

b. Carefully read the instructions on the web page. The sites will differ but normally you need to enter:

> **Vocab**
>
> A **site** is a website on the World Wide Web.

    i. details of your weight

    ii. details of the type of exercise, for example a brisk walk

    iii. how long you have exercised.

c. You will usually need to click on a button labelled 'Calculate' or something similar.

d. The number of calories will then be shown. For example:

    calories burnt = 271

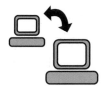

e. Compare different types of exercise such as walking and running.

f. Close the browser and switch off the computer system.

2. Use electronic displays to find information

> **ICT Skill for Life standard**
>
> These tasks help you to practise:
>
> ■ recognising and using appropriate sources of ICT
>
> ■ finding information from an ICT-based source using appropriate facilities.

Information is often presented on some type of electronic display. For example:

railway station – train arrivals, departures and times

digital television – information about programmes

DVD – the contents of the disk.

Railway station

When you are next in a railway station, consider the information that is displayed in different places.

a. Compare how the information is shown in different places. Look at the platform display, the main station information board displays and the arrival and departure monitor displays.

b. Which information is duplicated? How is it presented? What information is only shown on particular displays?

c. If you wanted to check the time of a train, which source would you use?

Digital television

The digital television remote controls enable you to find out additional information about the programmes.

a. Using the remote control, find a description of the programme you are watching and information on alternative programmes on other channels.

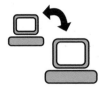

b. Explore the options and find information on other choices of programme later in the day.

c. Clear the information from the screen.

d. Select a 24-hour news channel and consider the way further information is added to the display. The information is sometimes shown on a single line that scrolls across the screen so you need to watch it to read the whole message.

e. Switch off the television.

DVD

Using the DVD remote control, explore a DVD of your choice to gain an understanding of the options it provides and the information it contains.

a. Use the menu to make selections.

b. See how the information is presented to you, for example with choices of language and parts of the film.

c. Continue until you are confident that you can find any information you need.

d. Close the system.

Leisure

1. Planning a trip to the cinema or theatre

ICT Skill for Life standard

This task helps you to practise:

- recognising and using appropriate sources of ICT

- finding information from an ICT-based source using appropriate facilities.

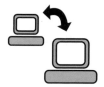

The World Wide Web can be a very useful resource when you are planning to visit the cinema or the theatre. Many venues have websites with information about what is playing now and in the future. In some cases, you can even buy your tickets online.

a. Ask a friend, colleague or your tutor to provide you with the address of the website of a local cinema or theatre. For example:

Nottingham Showcase cinema: www.showcasecinemas.co.uk/pages/nottingham.phtml

Nottingham Royal Centre theatres: www.royalcentre-nottingham.co.uk

b. Enter the address into your browser and visit the site.

c. Study the opening page of the site and try to find the option for what is showing tomorrow. Select a film and find the times for the next two days. Alternatively, find out what is playing at the theatre this week and next month. You may need to scroll up and down the page to find the information.

d. Some sites will provide information about the film or show. Try to find out if the film or show would interest you.

e. Websites often contain further information, such as details about films or shows. Explore the options to find out if you can buy tickets online. You can retrace your steps by using the Back button in the browser.

f. Continue until you are confident you can find the information you need.

g. Close the browser and switch off the computer.

2. Send a postcard

> **ICT Skill for Life standard**
>
> This task helps you to practise:
>
> ■ using ICT to communicate.

Many websites allow you to send a free e-postcard. This is essentially a picture postcard and message sent as an email.

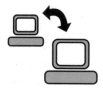

a. Ask a friend, colleague or your tutor to provide you with an address of a website offering free e-postcards. For example:

Mencap: www.mencap.org.uk/html/ePostcards/index.asp

Durham Local Authority: http://www.durham.gov.uk/durhamcc/ecards.nsf/ecard/epostcard

South Bedfordshire Local Authority: www.southbeds.gov.uk/places-to-go/epostcards.html

b. Enter the website address into a browser such as Microsoft Internet Explorer®.

c. Complete the online form. This will normally ask you to give:

- your name
- your email address
- the name of the person you are sending the postcard to
- your friend's email address
- your message.

Send a postcard to a friend or family member who has access to email.

d. Once you have completed the details of your message, follow the instructions displayed. This usually involves clicking on the 'Next' or 'Send' button.

e. In some cases, you will be shown a preview of your postcard.

f. Close the browser and switch off the computer.

Education and training

1. Wikipedia

ICT Skill for Life standard

This task helps you to practise:

- recognising and using appropriate sources of ICT
- finding information from an ICT-based source using appropriate facilities.

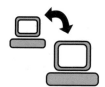

There are times when you need to find out the meaning of a word or some other information, perhaps to help your children with their education or to solve a crossword puzzle. Wikipedia is an online encyclopaedia with a difference – anyone can edit the information. A 'wiki' is the general term for an online product where users can edit the contents.

a. Ask a friend, colleague or your tutor to find the address of an online encyclopedia website such as Wikipedia – http://en.wikipedia.org/wiki/Main_Page

b. Enter the address into a browser and open the website.

c. Explore the Wikipedia webpage (see Figure 4.4). Try to identify the different options/links. If you run your mouse pointer over a link, it will change

Figure 4.4 Wikipedia

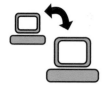
shape to a hand and the option may be underlined. Use the scroll bars so that you can see everything on the page.

d. Select an option that interests you and click on the link. The display will change. Again, select a subject that interests you and follow the link. Carry on discovering information about your topic.

For example, I selected the option 'History' and the display changed to show a variety of topics. I needed to scroll down the page to see all the content. I was interested in a small image of the American Dust Bowl and I clicked on it. The image enlarged and provided me with information about where it was taken. I used the 'Back' button to return to the original page.

e. If you need to retrace your steps, click on the Back button.

f. Continue exploring until you are satisfied that you have found enough information for your purpose and that you understand how to use Wikipedia to find content.

g. Print pages that interest you using the File menu, Print option and OK button.

h. Close the browser and switch off the computer.

You may have already used a printed encyclopaedia, but if you have not then arrange to visit your local library. Find the same subject in the printed encyclopedia and compare the printed information with that shown on your screen. How is the printed information presented? Does it agree with the information on screen?

Extra task

Visit Wikipedia again and find out how you could edit the contents of an entry. Consider how the information shown in Wikipedia differs from that shown in a printed encyclopedia.

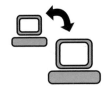

2. CD-ROM- and DVD-based information

> **ICT Skill for Life standard**
>
> This task helps you to practise:
>
> - recognising and using appropriate sources of ICT
>
> - finding information from an ICT-based source using appropriate facilities.

Thousands of CD-ROM and DVD disks have been published to distribute information. They cover a wide range of topics and issues. Choose one that you are interested in. Your local library may have CD-ROMs and DVDs that you can borrow.

> **Vocab**
>
> **Install** means to copy instructions on to the computer, in this case from a disk, so that it can read the information or application on the disk.

a. Ask a friend, colleague or your tutor to load the CD-ROM or DVD on to a computer. In some cases, the disks need to be installed.

b. All disks are designed in different ways. However, many disks will provide an introduction that explains how to use them or gives you a menu of choices.

c. Explore the opening displays and work through any introduction, or decide which menu option to select.

d. Find the topic that interests you and read the material. Some disks will offer you the option of printing the content. Print the materials if they will be useful to you and if a printer is attached to the computer.

e. CD-ROMs and DVDs often contain 'multimedia' which means sound and video. Ask your friend, colleague or tutor to ensure that the computer is set up so that you can listen and watch multimedia.

f. Many disks provide controls for you to play the video or listen to the audio. These often resemble the controls on a video player. Explore the controls and play, pause and replay any multimedia provided.

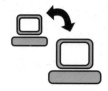

g. Continue to explore the information until you have found everything you need and you are confident that you can use a disk to find information.

h. Exit from the disk.

i. Switch off the computer.

Summary

Here are some useful tasks for you to do:

- Consider where information is likely to be available. For example, on a website, a CD-ROM or an electronic display board.

- Explore the display of information in order to identify all the options available to you.

- Compare the different ways that information is presented.

- Practise sending emails and text messages.

- Practise filling in online forms. Accuracy is vital when completing email addresses and other online information.

5 Entry Level 2: Developing and presenting information

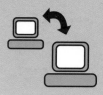

Objectives

This chapter will help you to:

- enter information and edit it
- check content and correct errors
- present information that is fit for a purpose.

Qualifications

This chapter will help you if you are studying for a qualification awarded by:

- OCR
- City and Guilds
- Edexcel.

Assessment

Each qualification is assessed through assignments. These are practical tasks that relate to your use of ICT. The details of the assessment vary between the awarding bodies so ask your tutor for details.

Applications

There are many computer applications designed to help you to present and edit information. In earlier chapters you have been introduced to:

- word processing – Microsoft Word®
- spreadsheets – Microsoft Excel®
- drawing – Microsoft Windows Paint®.

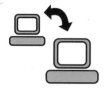

These applications help you to present words, numbers and pictures. There are also applications that will enable you to edit digital images that you have taken with a digital camera. Figure 5.1 shows Microsoft Photo Editor®. This application allows you to edit a photograph. As well as

Vocab

Edit means to make changes. For example, to remove part of a photograph.

providing several special effects that you can use, it lets you crop the image to remove parts that you don't want, resize the picture and rotate it. There are also various other features. At Entry Level 2 you are only asked to present, edit and check information in the form of words and numbers. You do not have to edit a photograph.

Figure 5.1 Microsoft Photo Editor®

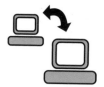

Correcting errors

One of the main advantages of computer applications is that you can correct any errors without having to start your document again from the beginning. There are several ways to do this:

1. Position the cursor. The correcting features of word processors and spreadsheets work according to the position of the cursor. This is the small flashing line on the screen that indicates where characters will be entered when you press a key. To move the cursor you need to use the mouse and mouse pointer. Place the mouse pointer at the new position and press the left mouse button. The cursor will move to the new position.

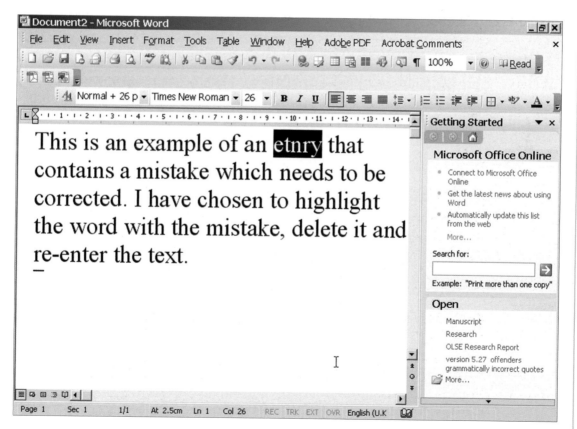

Figure 5.2 Highlighted text

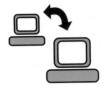

2. Delete text. The keyboard contains two delete keys:

- 'Backspace' key. When you press it, the 'Backspace' removes the character to the left of the cursor. This enables you to remove the last items you have entered.

- 'Del' key, meaning delete. This removes the character to the right of the cursor.

3. Highlight. To highlight a word or number, place the mouse pointer at the start or end of the item and hold down the left mouse button. Then move the pointer to the end or beginning. Now release the mouse button. You will see the background changes colour from white to black. If you press either the 'Backspace' or 'Del' key, the item will be removed (see Figure 5.2).

4. Insert a new item. When you reposition the cursor, you can enter text from the keyboard and it will appear at the new location.

Spelling and grammar checker

Many computer applications have a spelling and grammar checker built into them. These check the spelling and grammar of words that you have entered. The checker finds words that it thinks are misspelt and it finds potential problems with grammar. Checkers will, however, sometimes be wrong, and you are given the opportunity to agree or not with the suggested change.

Microsoft Word's® Spelling and Grammar checker can be set to check the spelling and grammar as you enter the words. It shows spelling mistakes by underlining the word in red and grammatical errors by underlining the word in green. When you are ready to check for errors, select the Spelling and Grammar option from the Tools menu.

Figure 5.3 shows the Microsoft Word® Spelling and Grammar checker. It shows in red what it believes to be a spelling mistake: 'etnry'. It offers three alternative spellings in the 'Suggestions' box. To select a suggestion, you need to double-click on it and it will be inserted in the text. If you do not agree there is an error, then you click on the Ignore Once or Ignore All button.

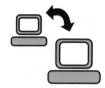

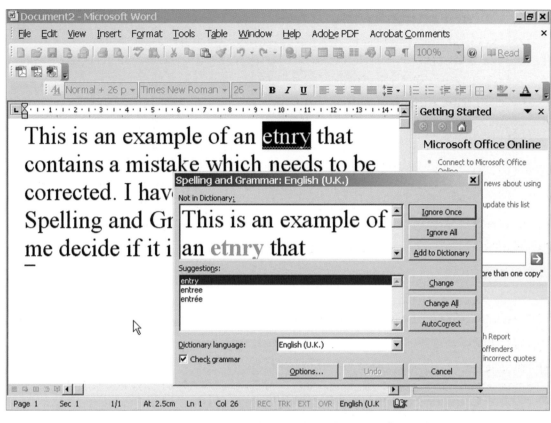

Figure 5.3 Microsoft Word® Spelling and Grammar checker

Practical tasks

This section contains a variety of tasks. They allow you to practise many of the skills required in Entry Level 2 'Developing and presenting information'. You can do the tasks in any order, and it is not necessary to complete them all. The tasks also provide opportunities to use ICT systems and to find and exchange information. They are therefore relevant to the standards covered in Chapters 3 and 4 as well.

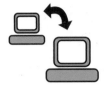

Citizen and community

1. Write a notice

> **ICT Skill for Life standard**
>
> This task helps you to practise:
>
> - entering information and editing it
> - checking content and correcting errors
> - presenting information that is fit for a purpose.

There may be occasions when you will need to write a short notice. For example, you may want to give instructions to the last person leaving the community centre, or you may want to let people know about a competition or trip. Select a type of notice that you may need to write.

a. Open Microsoft Word®.

b. Explore the application. Try to identify the menu, toolbars, scroll bars and cursor. Try to find the <u>S</u>pelling and Grammar checker on the <u>T</u>ools menu.

c. Write your notice. For example:

> If you are the last person to leave, please check that all the windows are shut and the lights have been turned off.

or

> On Saturday 23 September, we have organised a trip to Chatsworth House. If you would like to take part, please contact Dorothy.

d. Carefully read your notice and correct any errors using the 'Backspace' and 'Delete' keys.

e. If you are confident, use the <u>S</u>pelling and Grammar checker.

f. .... menu, <u>P</u>rint option and OK

g. .... your work with a meaningful

h. C............................ mputer.

2. Cr............................

ICT S............................

This t............................

■ en............................

■ pre............................ e.

There ma.......................... will need to produce a sign. For example, signs with arrows to direct people to a jumble sale, signs for the toilets or the car park.

a. Open Microsoft Windows Paint®.

b. Create a sign for a task you are involved in. Figure 5.4 shows my example of a car park sign.

c. Carefully check your sign and correct any errors by using the eraser tool and starting again.

d. Check that your computer is connected to a printer. Print your sign by clicking on the <u>F</u>ile menu, <u>P</u>rint option and OK button.

e. Ask a friend, colleague or your tutor to save your work with a meaningful file name such as 'Car park'.

f. Close Microsoft Windows Paint® and switch off the computer.

Vocab

Eraser tool is essentially an electronic rubber that lets you rub out parts of a drawing.

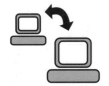

Figure 5.4 Car park sign

Economic activity, including paid and unpaid work

1. Electronic diary entry

ICT Skill for Life standard

This task helps you to practise:

- entering information and editing it
- checking content and correcting errors
- presenting information that is fit for a purpose.

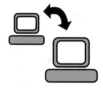

Keeping a diary is part of many people's jobs. Electronic diaries are now widely used. In this task you are asked to record your appointments for a day. These can be your work appointments or other tasks.

a. Open Microsoft Outlook® at the 'Calendar' page. Microsoft Outlook® is an application designed to help you organise your working life. It offers an email system, appointments diary and several other features.

b. Enter your appointments, tasks and other work for a day. Figure 5.5 shows an example of a day.

Figure 5.5 Diary

c. Carefully check your entries and correct any errors by using the 'Backspace' and 'Delete' keys.

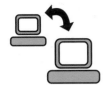

d. Check that a printer is connected to your computer. Print the diary page. To print your diary, select the File menu, Print option and OK button.

e. Close the application and switch off the computer.

2. Use a spelling checker to find errors

> **ICT Skill for Life standard**
>
> This task helps you to practise:
>
> ■ checking content and correcting errors.

Many readers judge individuals on the quality of their written work. Word processors provide 'spelling checkers' to help find mistakes in written work. Ask a friend, colleague or your tutor to provide a Microsoft Word® document for you to use.

a. Ask your tutor, friend or colleague to help open the document provided in Microsoft Word®. Figure 5.6 shows an example.

b. Check the spelling of the document using the Spelling and Grammar checker. This is found in the Tools menu.

c. Accept or ignore each suggestion. My example has three mistakes:

prt – part

listners – listeners

sigt –sight

d. Close Microsoft Word® and switch off the computer.

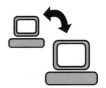

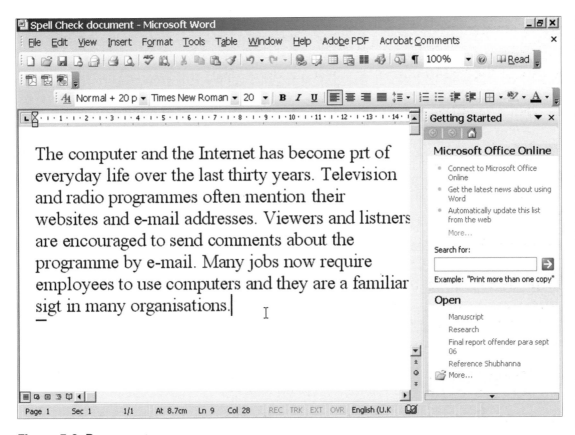

Figure 5.6 Document

Domestic and everyday life

1. Write a list

ICT Skill for Life standard

This task helps you to practise:

■ entering information and editing it

■ checking content and correcting errors

■ presenting information that is fit for a purpose.

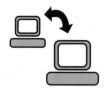

Life, at times, seems to centre on lists. There are shopping lists, things-to-do lists, lists of items to take on holiday, and many more. This task asks you to create a list that you need. The example in Figure 5.7 is a list of people who have volunteered to help at the refreshment stall for the community fête.

a. Open Microsoft Excel®. Microsoft Excel's® grid structure helps with the laying out of a complex list.

b. Create your list. An example is shown in Figure 5.7.

c. Carefully check your list. Notice and correct any errors by clicking in the spreadsheet cell and re-entering the item. This will remove the original entry.

d. Print your list by clicking on the File menu, Print option and OK button.

e. Ask a friend, colleague or your tutor to save your work with a meaningful file name such as 'List'.

f. Close Microsoft Excel® and switch off the computer.

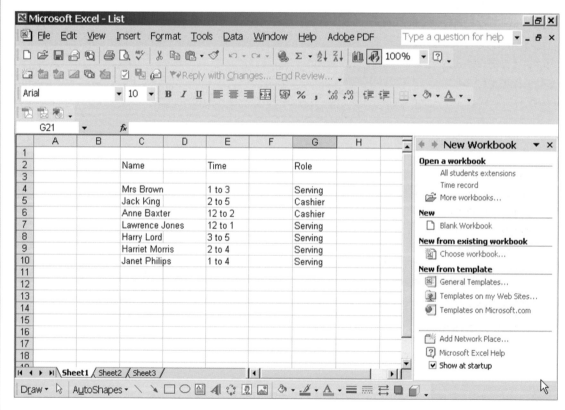

Figure 5.7 List

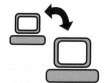

2. Send comments on a television or radio programme

Many television and radio programmes encourage viewers and listeners to send comments about the programmes using email. If you visit a programme's website, you will find a link to an email as one way to contact the programme. Figure 5.8 shows a typical email layout.

a. Ask a friend, colleague or your tutor to find a television or radio programme website of your choice. Open the email system.

ICT Skill for Life standard

This task helps you to practise:

- entering information and editing it
- checking content and correcting errors
- presenting information that is fit for a purpose.

Name

Email address

Comments

[Send] [Clear]

Figure 5.8 Email

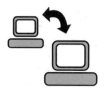

b. Complete the email form and add your comments about the programme.

c. Carefully check the form and correct any errors by clicking in the boxes and using the 'Backspace' and 'Delete' keys.

d. Send the email by clicking the <u>S</u>end button.

e. Close your browser and switch off the computer.

Leisure

1. Ask for holiday information

> **ICT Skill for Life standard**
>
> This task helps you to practise:
>
> - entering information and editing it
> - checking content and correcting errors.

There are many websites that provide information about holidays. Some of them allow you to:

- ask for extra information
- register for special offers
- ask for a brochure
- request a copy of the newsletter.

This involves filling in a form that asks for your name, postal address and email address.

a. Ask a friend, colleague or your tutor to find a web page that allows you to request information about holidays that interest you. For example:

www.thomson.co.uk

www.virginholidays.co.uk/my/newsletter

www.cosmos.co.uk/brochures.php

www.saga.co.uk/travel/General3/brochureOrder.asp

www.cunard.co.uk

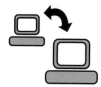

First name	
Surname	
House number	
Street	
Town	
Country	
Telephone number	
Email address	

Figure 5.9 Holiday information form

b. Open your browser and enter the website address to open the site.

c. Figure 5.9 shows the type of form that you will need to complete to receive more information. Enter your details on the form.

d. Check each entry on the form for mistakes. Correct mistakes by using the 'Backspace' and 'Delete' keys.

e. Send the form by clicking on the Submit button. In some cases, this may have a different name such as 'Send'.

f. Close the website and switch off the computer.

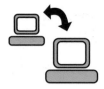

2. Create a holiday packing list

It is important when going away from home to make sure that you have all your clothes and other belongings with you. Making a list of what you need to pack will help you to remember everything.

ICT Skill for Life standard

This task helps you to practise:

- entering information and editing it
- checking content and correcting errors
- presenting information that is fit for a purpose.

a. Open Microsoft Word®.

b. Enter the details of your holiday list into the word processor. Figure 5.10 shows an example of a holiday packing list.

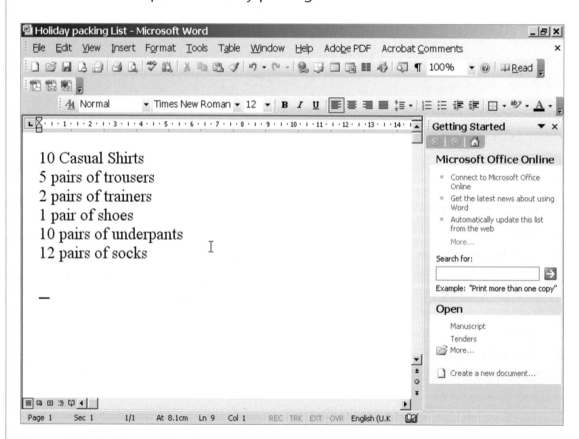

Figure 5.10 Holiday packing list

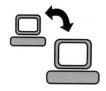

c. Carefully check your holiday list and correct any errors by using the 'Backspace' and 'Delete' keys.

d. Check that the computer is linked to a printer. Print your list by clicking on the File menu, Print option and OK button.

e. Ask a friend, colleague or your tutor to save your work with a meaningful file name such as 'Holiday packing list'.

f. Close Microsoft Word® and switch off the computer.

Education and training

1. Write a short note

There are many times when you need to write a note. Some examples include:

> **ICT Skill for Life standard**
>
> This task helps you to practise:
> - entering information and editing it
> - checking content and correcting errors
> - presenting information that is fit for a purpose.

- to let the school know your child is ill
- to remind yourself when a training course starts
- to find out if a friend is going to enrol on the course at the community centre.

a. Open Microsoft Word®.

b. Write a short note. For example:

c. Carefully check your note and correct any errors by using the 'Backspace' and 'Delete' keys.

> Dear Mrs Smith
>
> Linda is not well today so she is unable to come to school. I have made an appointment for her to see the doctor. I will let you know what the doctor says.
>
> Best wishes
>
> Jayne Collins.

d. Check that your computer is connected to a printer. Print your note by clicking on the File menu, Print option and OK button.

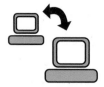

e. Ask a friend, colleague or your tutor to save your work with a meaningful file name such as 'School'.

f. Close Microsoft Word® and switch off the computer.

2. Reply to an email sent by a teacher

Schools and colleges often use email to communicate with you.

> ### ICT Skill for Life standard
>
> This task helps you to practise:
>
> - entering information and editing it
> - checking content and correcting errors
> - presenting information that is fit for a purpose.

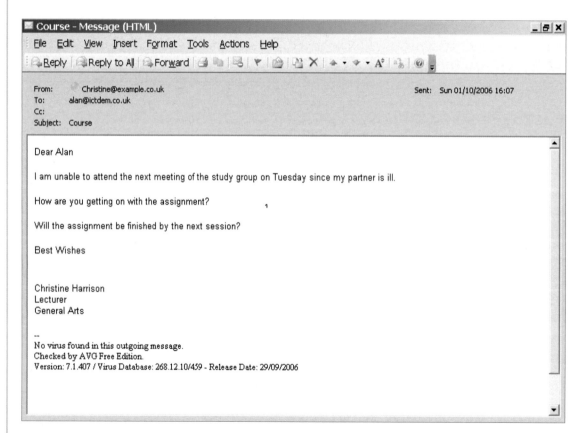

Figure 5.11 Receiving an email

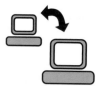

a. Ask a friend, colleague or your tutor to send you an email about your course. Open Microsoft Outlook® so that you can receive the message and reply to it. Figure 5.11 shows an email message that I have received. Figure 5.12 shows my reply to the message.

b. Write a reply to your message. The first step is to click on the Reply button and then enter your message.

c. Check your reply for mistakes. Correct them by using the 'Backspace' and 'Delete' keys.

d. Send the reply by clicking on the Send button.

e. Close Microsoft Outlook® and switch off the computer.

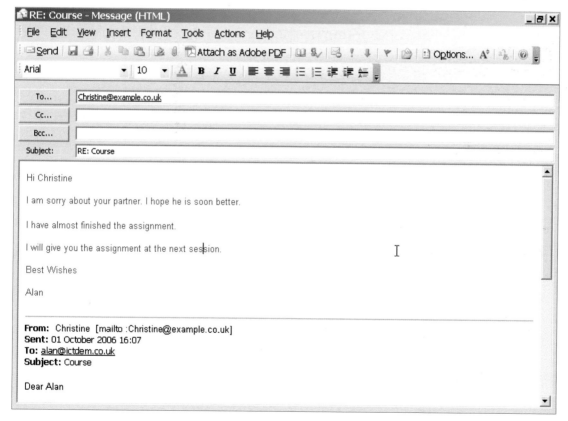

Figure 5.12 Replying to an email

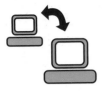

Summary

Here are some useful tasks for you to do:

- Practise entering information from the keyboard.

- Practise filling in online forms.

- Practise presenting information using different applications such as Microsoft Word®, Excel® and Windows Paint®.

- Carefully check your work for mistakes.

- Correct your mistakes using the 'Backspace' and 'Delete' keys.

- Use the spelling and grammar checker to identify and correct possible errors.

- Check that your work is going to achieve your aim.

Objectives

This chapter will help you to:

- use correct procedures to start and shut down ICT systems and to open, close and use applications as appropriate
- use input devices
- use software applications to achieve a purpose
- recognise and use interface features
- understand that settings can be adjusted according to individual needs
- work with files to enable the storage and retrieval of information
- insert and remove media
- follow recommended safe practices
- keep information secure.

Qualifications

This chapter will help you if you are studying for a qualification awarded by:

- OCR
- City and Guilds
- Edexcel.

Assessment

Each qualification is assessed through assignments. These are practical tasks that relate to your use of ICT. The details of the assessment vary between the awarding bodies so ask your tutor for details.

Start up

The first task you will need to do each time you use a computer is to switch it on. The process is:

1. Check that the computer and monitor are plugged into the power supply.

2. Switch on the monitor using the on switch. This is a button below the monitor screen. When you switch on the monitor, a small light will appear at the switch and sometimes you will hear a noise.

3. Switch on the computer. The on switch is normally positioned on the front of the computer. You should hear the internal fan start up and the monitor will start to show the boot-up sequence. This may not make a lot of sense, but it involves checking the different parts of the computer. You may see the drive lights flash on the computer as the system tests them.

4. After a few seconds, the word 'Windows' should appear and finally a display asking you to select your user name and enter a password. When you have successfully logged on by entering your user identification and password, you will see the Microsoft Windows® desktop appear (see Figure 3.17, page 47).

Shut down

Your final task each time you finish using the computer is to switch it off. This is not simply about pressing the off switch but requires you to follow the correct procedure. If you do not follow the procedure, there is a danger that you will damage any information stored on the computer. The switch-off procedure is part of safeguarding information or data. The procedure is:

1. Click on the Start button in the bottom left-hand corner of the Microsoft Windows® desktop and select the Turn Off Computer option (see Figure 6.1).

2. The 'Turn off computer' window will appear. Click on the Turn Off button (see Figure 6.2).

3. The words 'Microsoft Windows® is shutting down' will appear on the monitor and then the display will go blank. The noise of the computer drives and fan will stop. The lights on the front of the computer will switch-off.

4. The monitor light will still glow since you have not switched off the monitor. Press the on/off switch and the light will disappear.

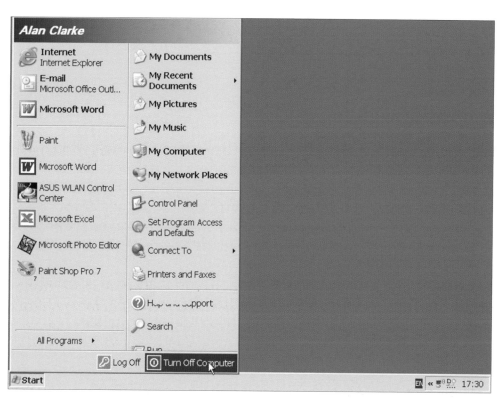

Figure 6.1 'Start' and 'Turn Off Computer'

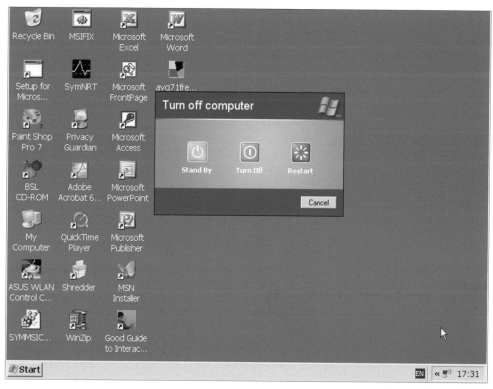

Figure 6.2 'Turn off computer' window

Open applications

Once the computer is switched on, the display shows the Microsoft Windows®
desktop. This is made up of a variety of small images called 'icons'. Some of the
icons represent applications such as Microsoft Word®. Other icons form links to
different parts of the computer system; these are called 'shortcuts'. If you
double-click on any of the application icons, they will open. Figures 3.4 and 3.5
show open Microsoft Word® and Excel® applications (see pages 27 and 28).

Applications are not always shown on the desktop, and there is an alternative
way to open them. You can select the Start button and highlight the
All Programs option to reveal a menu. If you then click on any of the
applications they will open.

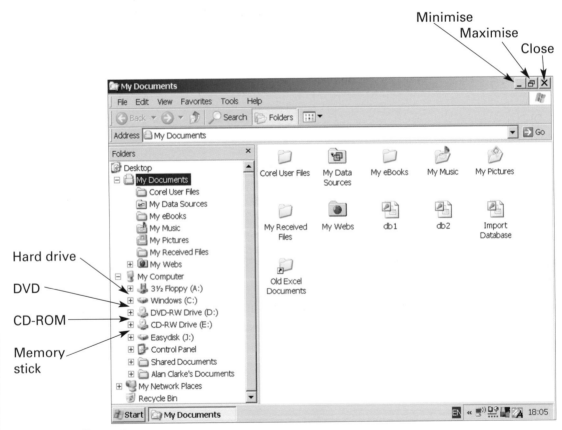

Figure 6.3 Controls

In the top right-hand corner of the application window is a group of controls (see Figure 6.3). These are:

- minimise
- maximise
- close.

'Minimise' reduces the display to an icon on the bottom bar of the desktop. If you click on the icon, it will return to full size. In some cases, the application occupies a window smaller than the whole screen. The 'maximise' control will change the display so that it fills the screen. The 'close' button shuts down the application.

You can have several applications open at the same time. You can use the 'minimise' button to clear the screen of applications, sending them to the bottom bar of the desktop, while still leaving them open.

Storage

Computers and other ICT devices store information in a variety of ways. For example, on:

- internal magnetic disks, often called the 'hard disk'
- CD-ROMs and DVDs – these look exactly the same as those used for music or films
- floppy disks
- memory cards – these are often used in digital cameras to store your pictures
- memory sticks – portable devices that you plug into a computer in order to transfer information.

Information stored in a computer is called a file, and you can have files that contain text, music, pictures or films. To help organise the files, you can keep them in folders that are normally grouped around a common theme. In Figure 6.3, you can see a folder containing e-books that is called 'My eBooks', a folder containing pictures that is called 'My Pictures', and some individual files such as 'db1' and 'db2'. Folders are shown with an icon of a folder, while file icons depend on what type of information they hold. Files with 'db' underneath the icon contain databases.

Vocab

A **file** is a collection of information, for example a letter.

A **folder** is a storage space that holds files.

A **database** is a collection of information stored on the computer in a way that makes it easy to find particular pieces of information.

You can also store folders inside one another. In Figure 6.3 you can see a folder called 'My Documents' that contains several other folders, for example 'Corel User Files'. This allows you to organise your folders and files. It is important to do this since within a few weeks of using a computer you can have hundreds of different files, and it can be difficult to find the one you need.

Saving

All Microsoft Office® applications provide an option that allows you to save a file. Figure 6.4 shows the 'Save As' window. You can save a file by clicking on the File menu and Save or Save As options. When you initially save a file, you click on Save and the 'Save As' window opens. Use this window to pick a folder in which to store your file. If you then make changes to your work, and want to save the changes, click on Save . The window will not open since the system

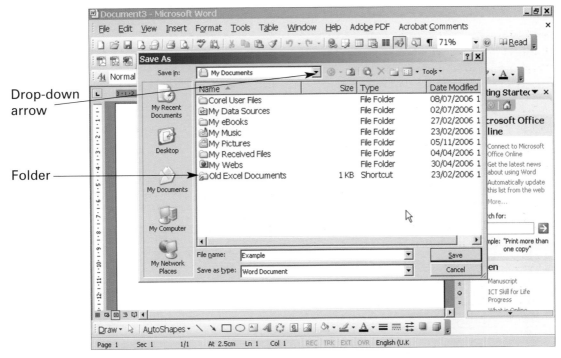

Drop-down arrow

Folder

Figure 6.4 'Save As' window

assumes that you want to save the file in the same folder and with the same name as you did initially. The alternative is to click on the Save As option which will always open the window. This allows you to save the same file with a different name or in a different folder.

In order to select a folder in which to save your file, you need to click on the drop-down arrow next to the 'Save in' box. This opens a list of folders and drives. If you click on a folder, its name will appear in the 'Save in' box. The drives are shown by a letter such as 'C:', which is the hard drive or disk, or 'A:', which is the floppy drive. Figure 6.5 shows the drop-down list.

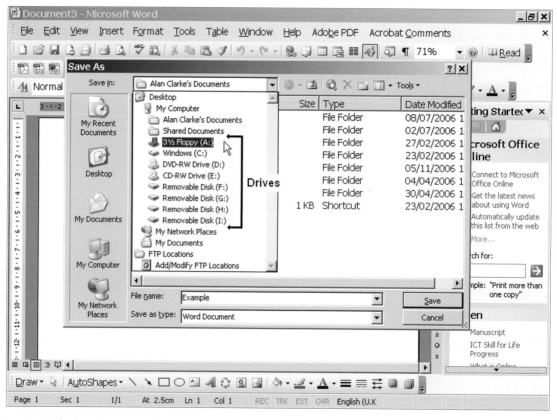

Figure 6.5 Drop-down list

Applications

Some computer applications help you to manage your files and folders. Microsoft Windows® comes with an application called Windows Explorer® that is accessed by pressing the Start button, highlighting All Programs and Accessories and clicking on Windows Explorer®. Figure 6.3 (page 94) illustrates Microsoft Windows Explorer®.

Practical tasks

This section contains a variety of tasks. They allow you to practise many of the skills required in Entry Level 3 'Using ICT systems'. You can do the tasks in any order, and it is not necessary to complete them all. The tasks also provide opportunities to find and exchange information and to develop and present information. They are therefore relevant to the standards covered in Chapters 7 and 8 as well.

Citizen and community

1. Using local authority services

> **ICT Skill for Life standard**
>
> This task helps you to practise:
>
> - using the correct procedures to start and shut down ICT systems and to open, close and use applications
> - using input devices and software applications to achieve a purpose
> - recognising and using interface features.

Local authorities provide many services via their websites. This task finds out what they can offer.

a. Switch on your computer and find your local council's website, for example www.rushcliffe.gov.uk

The website will present you with a range of services and information. On my website I can:

- report a problem such as graffiti, refuse collection or abandoned cars
- find out about planning and building applications
- pay bills
- apply for jobs
- find out about council tax
- calculate benefits
- find out about sports facilities
- email my Member of Parliament (MP).

b. Choose a service you need to use, such as reporting a problem with fly-tipping, and follow the instructions to successfully complete the task. You will need to make choices and enter information. Figure 6.6 shows the types of options you can choose between. I selected 'Planning permission' by clicking on the radio button.

c. Finish using the service and close the browser using the <u>F</u>ile menu and <u>C</u>lose option or the Close button in the right-hand corner of the browser.

d. Shut down Microsoft Windows® and switch off the computer.

Vocab

A **radio button** shows when an option is selected by placing a dot or tick in its centre. Figure 6.6 shows an example where 'Planning permission' is selected.

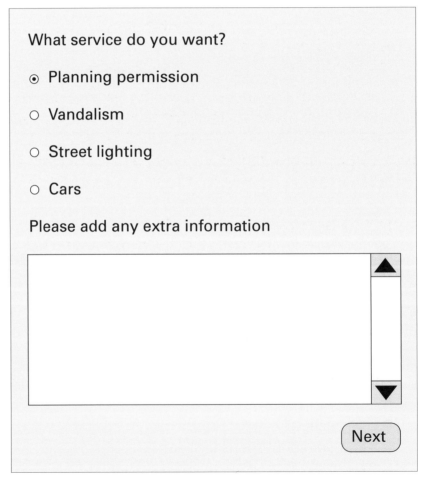

What service do you want?

⦿ Planning permission

○ Vandalism

○ Street lighting

○ Cars

Please add any extra information

Next

Figure 6.6 Choices

2. Find out about your Member of Parliament

> **ICT Skill for Life standard**
>
> This task helps you to practise:
>
> ■ using the correct procedures to start and shut down ICT systems and to open, close and use applications
>
> ■ using input devices and software applications to achieve a purpose
>
> ■ recognising and using interface features.

You may need to contact your Member of Parliament (MP). Many have email addresses so that you can send them a message. Some have websites with information about their interests available online.

a. Switch on your computer and find the parliament website: www.parliament.uk/directories/directories.cfm. This provides information about all MPs, including their email addresses.

b. Identify your own MP. Some will have their own websites with online biographies, and they will allow you to contact them by email. Find out about your MP.

c. Explore the website by moving through the site using the links and Forward and Back buttons. Try to identify what are the main interests of your MP, and how you can contact them.

d. Print any web pages that are useful to you.

e. Identify other MPs that interest you and find out more about them.

f. Close the browser using the File menu and Close option or the Close button in the right-hand corner of the browser.

g. Shut down Microsoft Windows® and switch off the computer.

Economic activity, including paid and unpaid work

1. Create an organisation chart

> **ICT Skill for Life standard**
>
> This task helps you to practise:
>
> - using the correct procedures to start and shut down ICT systems and to open, close and use applications
> - using input devices and software applications to achieve a purpose
> - recognising and using interface features.

Almost all organisations create charts to show their management structure. These are often called 'family trees' (see Figure 6.7).

a. Switch on your computer and open Microsoft Windows Paint®.

b. Create an organisation chart for your own employer, community group or a club that you belong to.

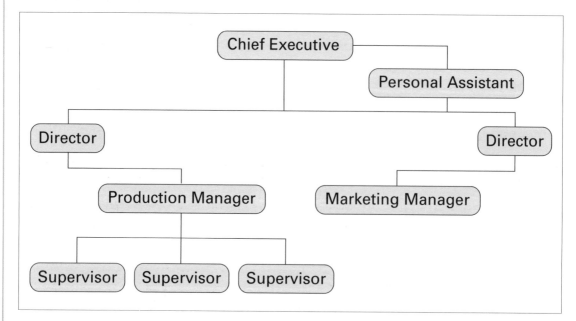

Figure 6.7 Organisation chart

c. Save your work onto a floppy disk, a memory stick or the internal hard drive. If you are able save the file onto two or more devices then compare the different ways.

d. When you have finished, close Microsoft Windows Paint®. Shut down Microsoft Windows® and switch off the computer.

2. Finding files and folders

> **ICT Skill for Life standard**
>
> This task helps you to practise:
>
> ■ using the correct procedures to start and shut down ICT systems and to open, close and use applications as appropriate
>
> ■ using input devices
>
> ■ recognising and using interface features
>
> ■ understanding that settings can be adjusted according to individual needs
>
> ■ working with files to enable the storage and retrieval of information.

Computers have now become an important part of business. Almost all organisations that use technology generate great numbers of files and folders of information. It is important to be able to find these files and folders. The Microsoft Windows® operating system has functions to search for files and folders.

a. Switch on your computer.

b. Find the Search option by using the Start menu (see Figure 6.1, page 93). Click the option to open the 'Search Results' window (see Figure 6.8).

c. Choose what you want to look for by clicking on one of the options. Figure 6.9 shows the window that opens if you select the Documents option.

d. Complete the search form by clicking on the radio buttons of your choice and entering the name of the document you are looking for. Click on the Search button. You should see that the space to the right of the search form starts to fill with documents that have been identified.

e. Check the documents that have been found to see if the one you want is there. The way that the file is shown depends on the view that has been selected. You can change the view by selecting the View menu on the menu toolbar. Five options will appear:

i. thumbnails

ii. tiles

iii. icons

iv. list

v. details.

Change the view by clicking on an option. Compare several until you find the one that helps you find the document you want.

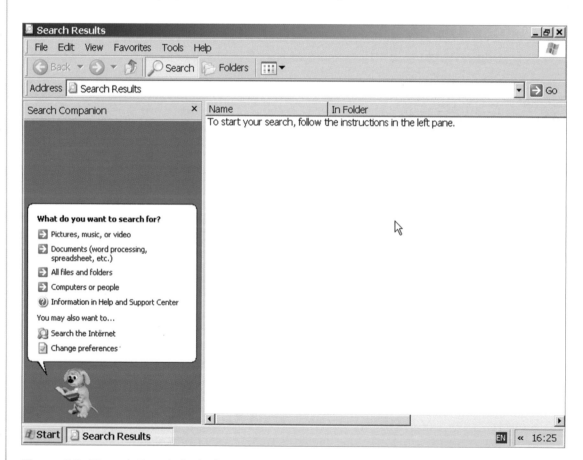

Figure 6.8 'Search Results' window

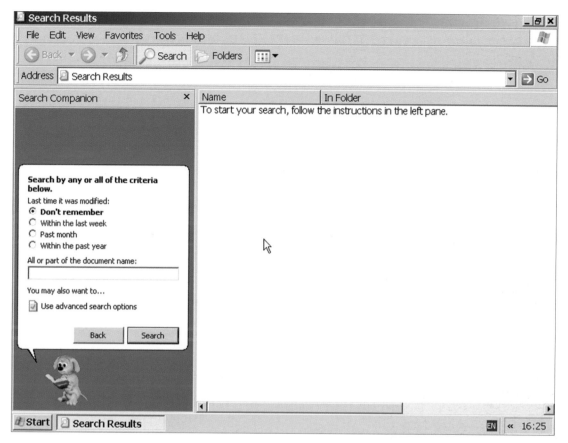

Figure 6.9 Searching for files and folders

f. To open a document, double-click on it. Once it is open you can check whether it is the correct one. To return to the search results, close the document window.

g. Once you have found the document you want, close the 'Search' windows.

h. Shut down Microsoft Windows® and switch off the computer.

Domestic and everyday life

1. Adjust the computer settings to meet your needs

> **ICT Skill for Life standard**
>
> This task helps you to:
>
> - understand that settings can be adjusted according to individual needs.

The computer display, outputs, keyboard and mouse can be adjusted to meet your own preferences and needs. For example, the mouse buttons can be changed for a left-handed user.

The settings are controlled by the Microsoft Windows® operating system through either the Control Panel or the Accessibility Options.

a. Switch on your computer.

b. Find the 'Control Panel' using the Start menu and Control Panel option. Figure 6.10 shows the 'Control Panel' in Microsoft Windows Professional XP®.

c. There are several options that let you make changes. These include:

> **Vocab**
>
> The **Control Panel** is a window in the Microsoft Windows® operating system. It provides ways to customise the computer system to your needs.
>
> **Accessibility Options** are about making the computer system more suitable for people to use.

- change the mouse for a left-handed user – 'Mouse' option
- make the mouse pointer easier to see – 'Mouse' option
- make the cursor more visible – 'Accessibility Options'
- make the display easier to read – 'Accessibility Options'.

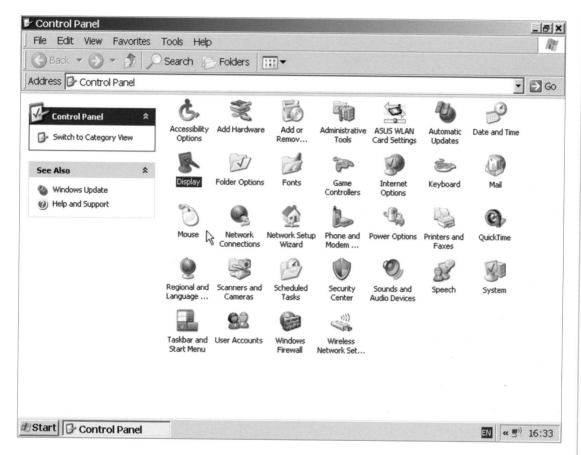

Figure 6.10 Control Panel

d. Click on the Mouse option to find out how you can change the way the mouse works. Figure 6.11 shows the 'Mouse Properties' window. Try to find the different options and consider if they would help you. If you want to make a change, ask a friend, colleague or your tutor to help. Close the window when you have finished.

e. To find out about other options, click on the Accessibility Options. Figure 6.12 shows the 'Accessibility Options' window. Try to locate the different options and consider if they would help you. If you want to make a change, ask a friend, colleague or your tutor to help. Close the window when you have finished.

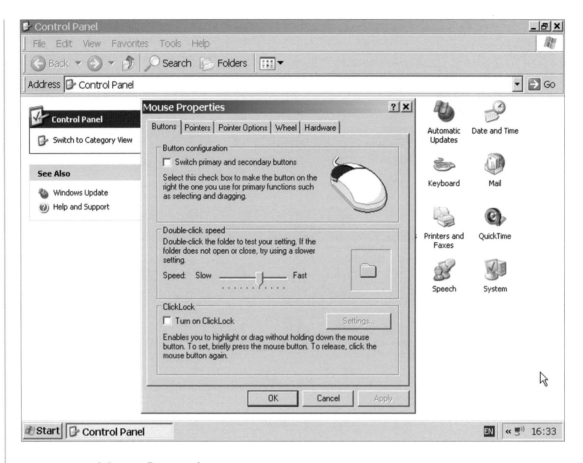

Figure 6.11 Mouse Properties

f. When you have finished, close the windows to return to the desktop. Shut down Microsoft Windows® and switch off the computer.

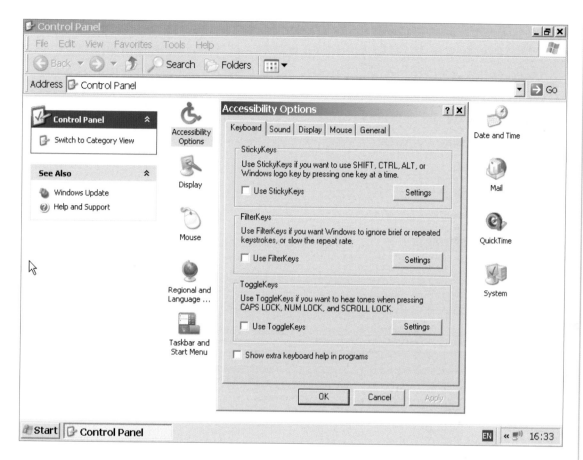

Figure 6.12 Accessibility Options

2. More about adjusting the computer settings to meet your needs

Another way that Microsoft Windows® provides help to users is through the 'Accessories' option in the 'All Programs' menu.

ICT Skill for Life standard

This task helps you to:

■ understand that settings can be adjusted according to individual needs.

a. Switch on your computer.

b. From the Start menu, highlight All Programs . Then highlight the Accessories and Accessibility options. Figure 6.13 shows the menus and options.

c. There are five 'Accessibility' options:

i. Accessibility Wizard

ii. Magnifier

iii. Narrator

iv. On-Screen Keyboard

v. Utility Manager.

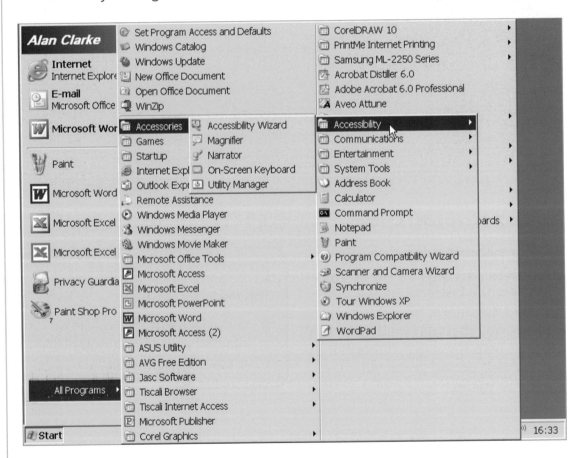

Figure 6.13 'Accessibility' options

Figure 6.14 Accessibility Wizard

d. The 'Accessibility Wizard' allows you to change the settings to meet your needs (see Figure 6.14). Click on the option. Answer the questions and follow the instructions. Ask a friend, colleague or your tutor to help if you need assistance.

e. Look at the effects of your changes.

f. When you have finished, close the windows to return to the desktop. Shut down Microsoft Windows® and switch off the computer.

Leisure

1. Take a photograph with a digital camera

There are many types of digital camera, but often each one will have features such as:

■ an on/off switch

■ a screen to show the photograph you are taking

■ a zoom

■ a memory card to store your pictures

■ a menu

■ control buttons

■ a photograph button

■ a video button.

For a small device, there are a lot of controls. However, if you examine your central-heating control box you will find many controls in a similar space.

a. Inspect the camera.

b. Can you see the following?

   i. an on/off switch

   ii. a small screen

   iii. controls – often indicated by small pictures or words, for example zoom and menu buttons

   iv. a button to take a photograph, normally on the top right-hand side of the camera.

c. Switch on the camera – the screen will light up and the shutter protecting the lens will open.

d. Take several photographs.

e. Check the quality of each image by finding the replay control or switch, sometimes indicates by a picture of an arrow. The control will allow you to look at each image in turn.

f. Change the image quality by using the 'Find' menu and the 'Image Quality' option. Photo quality is shown by a number such as '2MP' – 2 mega pixels. If you choose a higher number, the quality will improve. A lower number gives poorer quality. However, the camera can store fewer high-quality images than low-quality images so you need to decide what you need.

g. To practise, take some pictures of similar things.

h. Compare your different images. It is sometimes difficult to see the difference on the small screen. Delete the pictures you do not want to keep.

i. When you have finished, switch off the camera.

2. Print your digital pictures

Many supermarkets and photographic shops will print your pictures, or you can use a photographic printer to print your own.

> **ICT Skill for Life standard**
>
> This task helps you to practise:
>
> - using correct procedures to start and shut down ICT systems
> - recognising and using interface features
> - inserting and removing media.

a. Switch on the camera – the screen will light up and the shutter protecting the lens will open.

b. Remove the memory card from the camera.

c. Take the memory card to a supermarket or photographic shop. Insert the card into the self-service system for printing photographs and print your favourite images.

d. Alternatively, insert the memory card into a photographic printer and print your selected images.

e. Replace the memory card in the camera

f. Switch off the camera and printer.

Education and training

1. Find learning materials

> ### ICT Skill for Life standard
>
> This task helps you to practise:
>
> ■ using correct procedures to start and shut down ICT systems
>
> ■ recognising and using interface features
>
> ■ using input devices and software applications to achieve a purpose.

Many websites provide free learning materials. For example:

www.hodderclait.co.uk

www.bbc.co.uk/languages

a. Switch on your computer.

b. Connect your computer to the internet and open a browser.

c. Use a search engine to find a website that provides free learning materials. Figure 7.1 (page 119) shows the Google search engine.

> ## Vocab
>
> A **search engine** is a website that helps you to find web pages.

d. Look at the different sites until you find one that offers you useful learning materials. Figure 6.15 shows the Hodderclait website that provides learning resources if you are studying ICT.

e. Explore your chosen website to find suitable materials.

f. Explore the learning materials until you are confident that you know how they help can you.

g. Close the website and your browser.

h. Switch off the computer following the correct procedure.

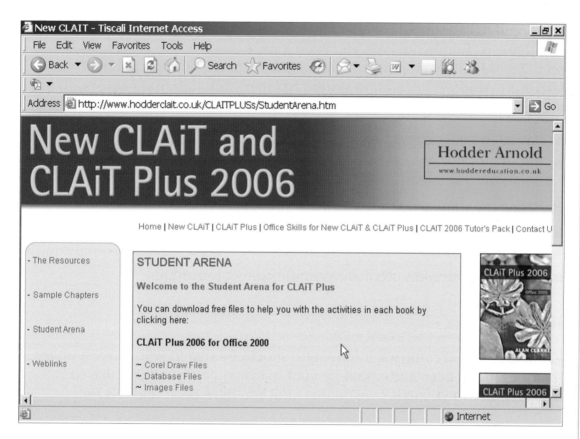

Figure 6.15 Hodderclait Student Arena

2. Using a tutorial

ICT Skill for Life standard

This task will help you to practise:

- using correct procedures to start and shut down ICT systems

- recognising and using interface features

- using input devices and software applications to achieve a purpose

- inserting and removing media.

The use of ICT to support people's learning is now a familiar part of education and training. Tutorials to help you learn a wide range of subjects are available on CD-ROMs and websites, and are built into computer applications. The Microsoft Windows® operating system has many tutorials that help you to use the Windows® system.

a. Switch on your computer.

b. Insert into the drive a CD-ROM that contains a tutorial on a subject that interests you.

c. Open the tutorial that the CD-ROM contains and study the material.

d. When you have completed enough of the material to meet your needs, close the tutorial.

e. Switch off the computer following the correct procedure.

Information

No customer and company information should be shared with anyone unless that person has been authorised by your manager. It is good practice to assume that everything is confidential until you have been told it is not.

Summary

Here are some useful tasks for you to do:

- Practise switching computers and other equipment on and off using the correct procedures.

- Practise opening and closing different computer applications.

- Practise using the operating system to change settings.

- Practise using different applications such as Microsoft Windows Explorer®.

- Practise using the keyboard and mouse or other input devices.

- Practise inserting and removing CD-ROMs and other media.

- Explore applications and operating systems to develop your understanding of how options and functions are presented.

- Practise saving and retrieving files.

- Always follow recommended safe practices.

- Never tell anyone your password or allow unauthorised people to see your personal or employer's information.

Entry Level 3: Find and exchanging information

Objectives

This chapter will help you to:

- select and use appropriate sources of ICT information and other forms of information
- use internet sources of information
- use appropriate search techniques to find required information
- select and use information
- access, read and respond appropriately to email
- create and send email.

Vocab

Required information means the information that you have been asked to find or that you need for your own purposes.

Qualifications

This chapter will help you if you are studying for a qualification awarded by:

- OCR
- City and Guilds
- Edexcel.

Assessment

Each qualification is assessed through assignments. These are practical tasks that relate to your use of ICT. The details of the assessment vary between the awarding bodies so ask your tutor for details.

Search engines

The World Wide Web contains hundreds of thousands of websites that have a wealth of useful information and services but it can still be difficult to find what you need. You can get a lot of help from friends and colleagues who will give you website addresses. In addition, advertising often includes organisations' websites. However, the main way to find things on the internet is through a search engine.

A search engine is a website. It looks for web pages matching words that you enter. Figure 7.1 shows Google, which is a major search engine. You enter your search terms into the box and click on Google Search, which then finds all the web pages that match your words. There are often thousands and even millions of matches, but if you explore the top ten or twenty you will often find what you are looking for. If that does not work, try using some alternative search terms.

Vocab

Search terms are words that you enter into a search engine when you want to find something on the internet. The words match the information you are looking for.

Search terms

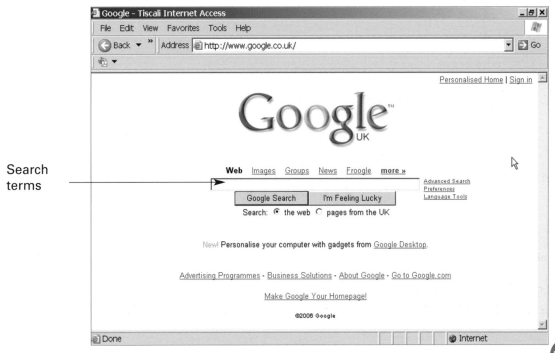

Figure 7.1 Google

Finding websites

Like many other things, using a search engine requires practice. The task below may help you to become familiar with them. It is based on using Google.

Searching

a. Switch on your computer, connect to the internet and open Microsoft Internet Explorer®, which is a type of application called a 'browser'.

b. Enter www.google.co.uk into your browser and you will access the Google search engine as shown in Figure 7.1

c. Enter some search terms relating to information that you want to find. For example:

> search term = Liverpool

This produced links to:

> football club
>
> university
>
> city council
>
> tourist information
>
> John Lennon airport
>
> museum
>
> theatre.

Search terms can be a single word or many words. It depends what you are looking for. For example, Liverpool weather, Liverpool railway station, Liverpool history world war.

d. If you run the mouse pointer down the list of web pages the search engine has given, you will see that it changes shape to a hand to indicate a link. If you click on a link then you will be taken to the selected web page.

e. Select a link and see what happens. For example:

> I chose Liverpool University and was linked to a page showing the courses available.

f. Return to the search engine by clicking on the Back button in the browser.

g. Scroll down the list of pages found. At the bottom you will notice a line saying 'Results Page 1 2 3 … Next'. This shows you that there are lots of other matches.

h. Click on Next and see a new set of matches appear.

i. Google offers other options such as 'Images' and 'News'. If you click on 'Images', you can search for pictures relating to your search terms. Clicking on 'News' lets you search for news items relating to your search terms.

j. Continue until you are confident that you can use the search engine.

k. Close the browser using the File menu and Close option and then switch off the computer using the correct procedure to safeguard your information.

Practical tasks

This section contains a variety of tasks. They allow you to practise many of the skills required in Entry Level 3 'Finding and exchanging information'. You can do the tasks in any order, and it is not necessary to complete them all. The tasks also provide opportunities to use ICT systems and to develop and present information. They are therefore relevant to the standards covered in chapters 6 and 8 as well.

Citizen and community

1. Filling in online forms

ICT Skill for Life standard

This task helps you to practise:

- selecting and using appropriate sources of ICT information and other forms of information

- using internet sources of information

- using appropriate search techniques.

The government and many companies increasingly provide services online.

a. Switch on the computer. Open Microsoft Internet Explorer® and find the search engine of your choice, for example www.google.co.uk. Search the World Wide Web for a service you wish to use. For example:

- renewing your car tax disc online
- buying a train ticket
- finding out about property prices, for example www.landreg.gov.uk/propertyprice
- reporting a problem to your local council, for example www.rushcliffe.gov.uk/doc.asp?cat=1558
- searching for a job.

b. Use the search engine to open the service website or enter the website address, for example www.direct.gov.uk/taxdisc

c. You can print each page of the process to keep a record of your actions. Use the File menu, Print option and OK button.

d. Read the information displayed on the website you have chosen and follow the instructions.

e. Enter the information you are asked for. Figure 7.2 illustrates an online form.

f. In some cases, you will be asked if you want to receive information about other services and products. Decide if you do or not.

g. If you are buying a service or product, you

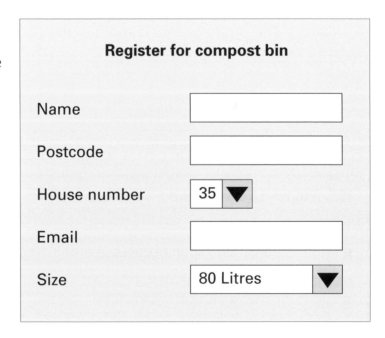

Figure 7.2 Online form

will have to enter debit or credit card information. Only go ahead if you are certain that the site is secure. You should read the information displayed about the security of the site, for example that all the information is encrypted so it cannot be read by other people.

h. At the end of the process you will see a summary of the transaction, usually with your address and details of your purchase. The summary may suggest that you print the page – do this in any case to keep a record of the transaction.

i. Close the browser using the <u>F</u>ile menu and <u>C</u>lose option.

j. Switch off the computer using the correct procedure.

Example

I renewed my car tax disc online. In order to do this you need your Vehicle Licence Application, which is called a 'V11'. You do not need your MOT or insurance documents. These are checked automatically by the system. On the computer, you enter the number from your tax disc renewal form or, alternatively, your logbook reference number and car registration. The website takes you through the process step by step. It tells you the details of your car so you can check if these are correct. You need to enter your debit or credit card details and the tax disc is sent to your home in the post.

2. Keeping in touch with new developments

> ### ICT Skill for Life standard
>
> This task helps you to practise:
>
> - selecting and using appropriate sources of ICT information and other forms of information
>
> - using internet sources of information
>
> - using appropriate search techniques
>
> - accessing, reading and responding appropriately to email
>
> - creating and sending email.

Many community organisations use email to keep people informed about new developments, meetings and activities. They send regular email updates to members in a similar way that you may receive a newsletter about local affairs through your door. Local authorities often offer the option of sending emails to inform you of local developments. For example:

email alerts to inform you about news stories that interest you: www.google.com/alerts?hl=en&q=&ie=UTF8

a local authority email alert service to keep you informed about local developments: www.rushcliffe.gov.uk/EmailSignup.asp?cat=8328

You will need to visit the local authority or community organisation website to register for email messages. The website will ask you what sort of information you want to receive.

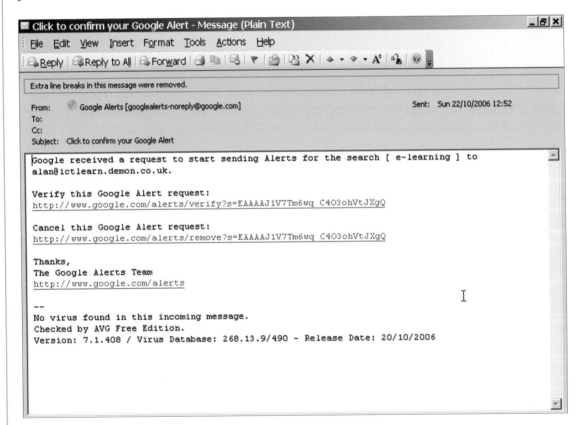

Figure 7.3 Google email alerts

An email alert system will often send you an initial email message to confirm that you want to go ahead. Figure 7.3 shows an email I received when I registered for the Google email news system.

a. Switch on and connect the computer to the internet.

b. Open Microsoft Internet Explorer®.

c. Use a search engine to find a relevant email alert service or enter the website address, www.google.com/alerts?hl=en&q=&ie=UTF8.

d. Read the information displayed. Follow the instructions to register to receive email messages about a subject that interest you.

e. Close Microsoft Internet Explorer®.

f. Check your email inbox and you will eventually receive an email from the service. Figure 7.3 shows the email from the Google news alert service.

g. The email will ask you to confirm that you want to receive email alerts or cancel the registration. Answer the email.

h. Close the email system.

i. Switch off the computer following the correct procedure.

Economic activity, including paid and unpaid work

1. Search for a job

> **ICT Skill for Life standard**
>
> This task helps you to practise:
>
> - selecting and using appropriate sources of ICT information and other forms of information
>
> - using internet sources of information
>
> - using appropriate search techniques.

Many organisations now advertise their vacancies on their websites, and newspapers offer online services to help you find jobs. In addition, several recruitment agencies work online. For example:

recruitment agencies: www.jobserve.com
www.totaljobs.com

vacancies in government departments: www.publicappts-vacs.gov.uk

The Guardian jobs: http://jobs.guardian.co.uk

The Telegraph jobs: http://jobs.telegraph.co.uk

Express and Star jobs: www.expressandstar.co.uk/jobs

a. Using a search engine, locate a newspaper, organisation or specialist recruitment agency website that could help you find a job.

b. Explore the website and find out what services they offer to help you search for a job. Examples of services include:

i. searching for current vacancies

ii. matching your CV against job advertisements

iii. giving advice on interviews

iv. helping you to write a CV.

c. Pick a service that is useful to you and use it. Figure 7.4 shows a job vacancy search service.

| Job title | ▼ |
| Key words | ▼ |

☐ Advertising   ☐ Health

☐ Construction   ☐ Information technology

☐ Catering   ☐ Mechanics

☐ Clerical   ☐ Retail

☐ Driving   ☐ Sales

☐ Engineering   ☐ Teaching

OK

Figure 7.4 Job vacancy search service

d. Choose another website and see how it can help you find a job.

e. Continue reviewing different websites until you are confident that you understand what is available to help you find a job.

f. Close the browser and the computer using the correct procedure.

Example

I registered for the 'Jobs by email' on the Guardian Jobs website (http://jobs.guardian.co.uk). Each week this sends me emails of jobs that match my needs. Some large organisations will also send emails when they have new vacancies.

2. Sending and receiving email

ICT Skill for Life standard

This task helps you to practise:

■ selecting and using appropriate sources of ICT information and other forms of information

■ using internet sources of information

■ using appropriate search techniques.

Email is now used on a large scale by many organisations. Lots of jobs now require you to use email to communicate with your colleagues, managers and customers. However, there are other forms of electronic communication. One is called a 'bulletin board'. This is when messages are posted onto a website rather than being sent to you. You can read the messages when you visit the site.

Some bulletin boards are called 'usenet groups'. These have been established to share information and discuss a shared interest. You can find out about them through search engines such as Google. For example:

Google groups: http://groups.google.co.uk

Microsoft groups: http://groups.msn.com

Yahoo groups: http://groups.yahoo.com

a. Switch on the computer and connect to the internet.

b. Open Microsoft Internet Explorer® and find a search engine that offers a way of finding groups, for example Google. Figure 7.1 (page 119) shows Google search. One of the options across the top of the search term box is 'Groups'. If you click on this option, a new page is displayed that lets you search for a group concerned with your interests.

c. Search for a group that deals with a subject of interest to you. Explore the list of groups presented and find one that you would like to join. Be aware some groups may discuss or share items that you might find offensive.

d. Join the group. You will often find a link called 'subscribe' that you need to follow. Read the instructions and they will tell you how to join.

e. Visit the group regularly and read what is sent to the bulletin board. When you are ready, make a contribution by sending your own message.

Domestic and everyday life

1. Home page

> **ICT Skill for Life standard**
>
> This task helps you to practise:
>
> ■ selecting and using appropriate sources of ICT information and other forms of information
>
> ■ using internet sources of information.

Many people find that they need to visit a particular website regularly because it keeps them up to date with a particular interest or with news in general. You can set your internet system so that each time you connect, it automatically opens your chosen website. This website becomes your 'home page'.

a. Choose a website that would be most useful for you to see each time you connect to the internet. You can choose your employer's website to keep up with the business, a news website to see the latest stories, your favourite football team's site, a search engine or any other website.

b. Identify the address of the website.

c. Switch on your computer. Click on the Start button and then the Control Panel option. Figure 6.1 (page 93) shows the 'Start' menu and Figure 6.10 (page 107) shows the 'Control Panel'.

d. Click on the Internet Options icon to reveal the 'Internet Properties' window as shown in Figure 7.5.

e. In the section 'Home page', enter a website address that you would like to visit. You can leave the entry blank, in which case your browser will display an empty screen when you connect to the internet.

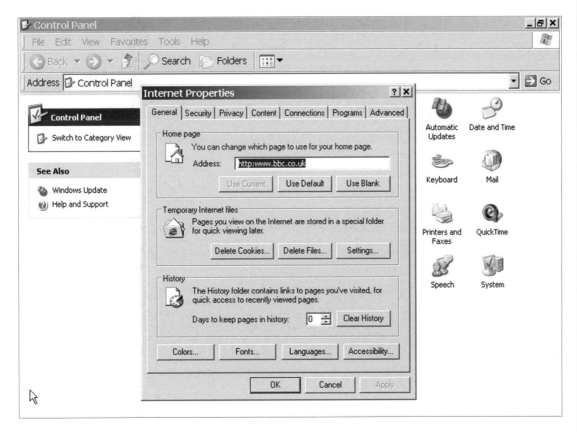

Figure 7.5 'Internet Properties' window

f. Connect your computer to the internet and your chosen website will automatically appear. If it does not then simply repeat steps **c**, **d** and **e**. The most likely error is to enter the website address incorrectly.

g. Experiment with different websites to find the most useful one for you.

h. Switch off the computer using the correct procedure.

2. Shop online

> ### ICT Skill for Life standard
>
> This task helps you to practise:
>
> - selecting and using appropriate sources of ICT information and other forms of information
>
> - using internet sources of information
>
> - using appropriate search techniques
>
> - selecting and using information.

One of the largest uses of the World Wide Web is shopping. People buy a wide range of products online, from holidays to books. One of the advantages of online shopping is that you can often read customer reviews of the products before buying.

a. Switch on the computer and connect to the internet.

b. Open Microsoft Internet Explorer® and find a search engine such as Google (www.google.co.uk).

c. Search for a product or for customer reviews of something you would like to buy. For example, a digital camera:

www.amazon.co.uk/electronics

www.cameras.co.uk/camera-reviews/nikon-coolpix-s9.cfm

www.dpreview.com

d. Visit two or three websites and compare the reviews provided for the same product.

e. What type of review is most useful to you?

f. Continue to find and read the reviews until you have enough information to decide if you want to buy the product.

g. You may find it helpful to print the web pages that have useful reviews.

h. Close your browser and switch off the computer following the correct procedure.

Extra task

Many online shopping sites encourage buyers to enter their own reviews. If you have bought a suitable product, enter a review on the shop website.

Leisure

1. Book tickets for the theatre, a show or a day out

ICT Skill for Life standard

This task helps you to practise:

■ selecting and using appropriate sources of ICT information and other forms of information

■ using internet sources of information

■ using appropriate search techniques

■ selecting and using information.

Many forms of entertainment are now advertised through websites. You can book tickets for many social activities online, for example the theatre, music concerts, sporting events and visiting the zoo. To do this:

a. Switch on the computer and connect to the internet.

b. Open Microsoft Internet Explorer® and find a search engine such as Google (www.google.co.uk).

c. Search for the website of a local theatre, sports club or other entertainment that you would like to attend. For example:

The National Theatre: www.nt-online.org

Nottingham Royal Centre: https://eticketing.co.uk/nottingham-royalcentre/default.aspx

Barcelona Football Club: www.barcelona.com/barcelona_tickets/fc_barcelona_football_tickets

d. Visit the website to see what shows or games are being performed. Decide what you would like to attend.

e. Find the booking page.

f. Book some tickets for an event. This will require entering your credit or debit card details. Figure 7.6 shows an example of a booking form for a theatre.

g. Print the web page that provides details of your booking.

h. The website will often provide details about travelling to the event that you may find useful to print out.

i. Close your browser and switch off the computer following the correct procedure.

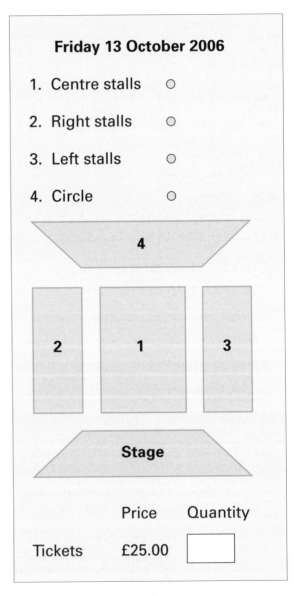

Figure 7.6 Booking tickets

Education and training

1. Visiting educational websites

> **ICT Skill for Life standard**
>
> This task helps you to practise:
>
> ■ selecting and using appropriate sources of ICT information and other forms of information
>
> ■ using internet sources of information
>
> ■ using appropriate search techniques
>
> ■ selecting and using information.

There are many websites that provide learning materials. You can visit the British Library and museums and art galleries through their websites, and these often have educational resources. For example:

The British Library: www.bl.uk

The British Museum: www.thebritishmuseum.ac.uk

NASA: www.nasa.gov/home/index.html?skipIntro=1

The Geography Site: www.geography-site.co.uk

The Internet Public Library: www.ipl.org

Moving Here: www.movinghere.org.uk

a. Switch on the computer and connect to the internet.

b. Open Microsoft Internet Explorer® and find a search engine such as Google (www.google.co.uk).

c. Search for a website of an educational resource or enter the address of one of the examples shown above.

d. Visit your chosen website and explore its options. Figure 7.7 shows the home page of the Moving Here website. This website offers a learning area with resources for teachers and learners. It also provides an online gallery of interesting items. You can register for a free newsletter and send an e-postcard to a friend.

e. Find resources on your chosen website that are useful for your own learning or for your family's learning, and study them.

f. Print the web pages that have useful content.

g. Continue to explore the website until you are sure that you have found everything that is useful.

h. Visit a new website and repeat the task.

i. Compare the resources and layouts of the two sites.

j. Close your browser and switch off the computer following the correct procedure.

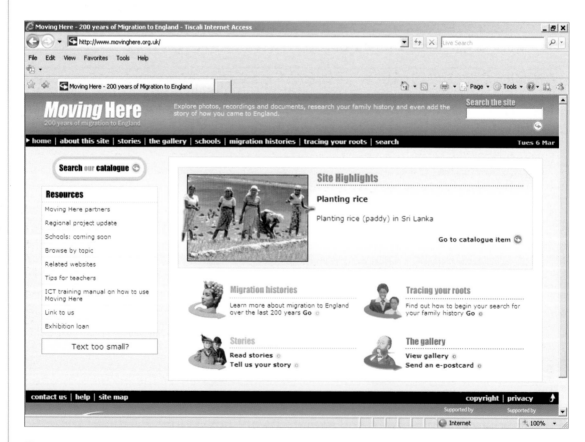

Figure 7.7 Moving Here

2. Email discussion group

> ### ICT Skill for Life standard
>
> This task helps you to practise:
>
> - accessing and reading emails
> - responding appropriately to emails
> - creating and sending emails.

Discussing issues is a useful way to learn. Many schools, colleges and other organisations use email to assist discussion. This allows groups of learners to carry on talking about a topic between teaching sessions.

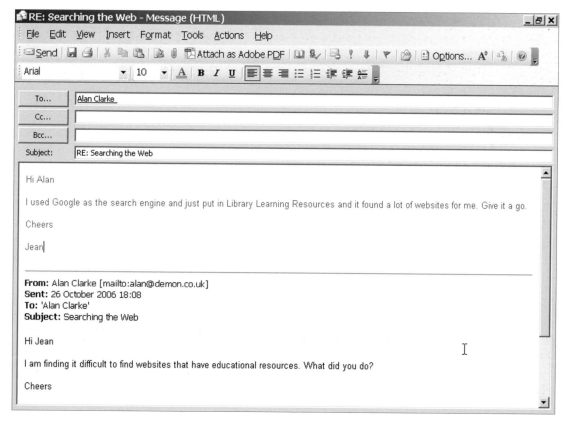

Figure 7.8 Replying to email

a. Ask the other learners in your class to share their email addresses with each other. This will allow you all to discuss what you are learning.

b. Switch on the computer and open Microsoft Outlook®.

c. Open the Mail task pane and then the 'New Mail' window by clicking on the New button.

d. Send messages to your colleagues about the course, and reply to any messages they send you.

e. Figure 7.8 shows an example of a reply to a message.

f. Continue to send and reply to messages.

Summary

Here are some useful tasks for you to do:

- Practise searching for information on websites using a search engine.

- Practise finding information on individual websites.

- Practise sending and replying to email.

- Practise selecting information from sources such as CD-ROMs and websites for a particular purpose.

8 Entry Level 3: Developing and presenting information

Objectives

This chapter will help you to:

- enter information using copy, cut, paste, drag and drop, undo and redo to achieve the required outcome
- align and justify text
- format text
- insert and position images to achieve a purpose
- enter and process numbers
- bring together information to achieve a purpose
- check meaning, accuracy and suitability
- present information that is fit for a purpose.

Qualifications

This chapter will help you if you are studying for a qualification awarded by:

- OCR
- City and Guilds
- Edexcel.

Assessment

Each qualification is assessed through assignments. These are practical tasks that relate to your use of ICT. The details of the assessment vary between the awarding bodies so ask your tutor for details.

Applications

Desktop publishing applications provide you with the means to create documents combining words, numbers and pictures, for example posters and leaflets. Figure 8.1 shows Microsoft Publisher®, which is a desktop publishing application.

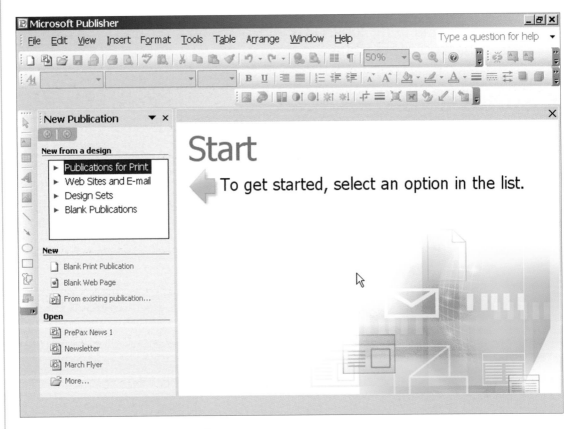

Figure 8.1 Microsoft Publisher®

Editing information

Microsoft Office® applications have many functions in common. These include copy, cut, paste, drag and drop, undo, redo, align (justify) and format text.

■ Copy – this function allows you to copy information and move it from one part of a document to another. You need to highlight the information – either text, numbers or images – select the <u>C</u>opy function, move the cursor to the new location and then select the <u>P</u>aste function. The copied information will appear at the new location. The original information is not changed.

- Cut – this function works in the same way as copy but with an important difference. The cut item is removed from its original location to the new one.
- Paste – this function is used with both copy and cut to paste the information into its new location.
- Drag and drop – this is a technique rather than a function. If you highlight some information and hold down the left mouse button, you can drag it around the page to a new location.
- Undo – this function will undo your last action.
- Redo – this function is used to correct a mistake you have made with undo.
- Align – this is a set of functions that allows you to align information.
    - Left align means that the information is presented in parallel with the left margin.
    - Right align means that the information is presented in parallel with the right margin.
    - Centre align means that the information is presented parallel with the centre line of the document.
    - Justify means that the information is presented with both left and right margins parallel.
- Format – this is a set of functions that allows you to change the characteristics of text.
- Bold – embolden text or numbers either by:
    - selecting the function and then entering the information
    or by
    - highlighting the information you want to embolden and then selecting the function.
- Underline – underline text or numbers either by:
    - selecting the function and then entering the information

or by

■ highlighting the information you want to underline and then selecting the function.

■ Italics – you can present text or numbers in italics either by:

■ selecting the function and then entering the information

or by

■ highlighting the information and then selecting the function.

Figure 8.2 shows the functions in Microsoft Word® but they are identical in other Microsoft Office® applications.

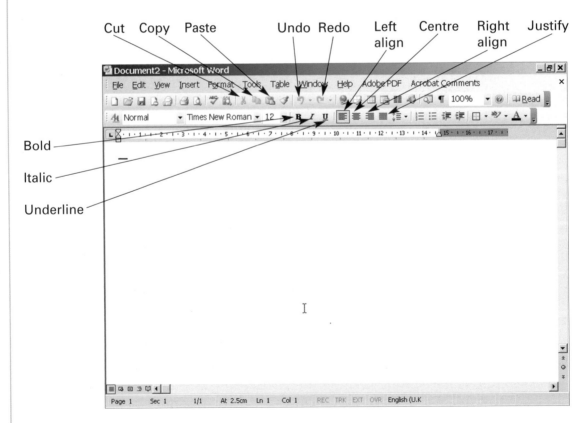

Figure 8.2 Functions

Practical tasks

This section contains a variety of tasks. They allow you to practise many of the skills required in Entry Level 3 'Developing and presenting information'. You can do the tasks in any order, and it is not necessary to complete them all. The tasks also provide opportunities to use ICT systems and to find and exchange information. They are therefore relevant to the standards covered in Chapters 6 and 7 as well.

Citizen and community

1. Leaflet

ICT Skill for Life standard

This task will help you to practise:

■ entering information using copy, cut, paste, drag and drop, undo and redo to achieve the required outcome

■ aligning and justifying text

■ bringing together information to achieve a purpose

■ checking meaning, accuracy and suitability

■ presenting information that is fit for a purpose.

There may be occasions when you need to produce a leaflet, for example to advertise a community event like a jumble sale. Microsoft Publisher® provides a wide range of templates to help you quickly create an attractive design.

a. Select an event or service that you want to advertise with a leaflet. For example, a community meeting, bring and buy sale or club meeting.

b. Switch on the computer and open Microsoft Publisher®. Select Publications for Print to change the display to Figure 8.3. This shows a variety of different layouts for a leaflet. Select one by double-clicking on it. A window called 'Personal Information' may pop up – close it by clicking on the X in the top right-hand corner of the window.

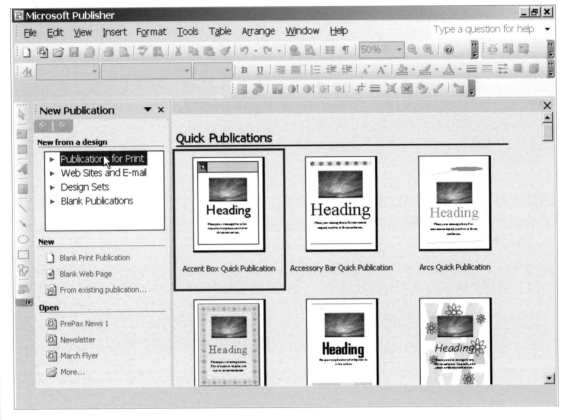

Figure 8.3 Microsoft Publisher® 'Publications for Print'

c. You will see your layout in the middle of the work area, as shown in Figure 8.4. On the left there are more alternatives based on your chosen design. Explore them until you find one that you like.

d. In the design there are two areas called 'Heading' and 'Place your message here'. These enable you to enter your own heading and message. If you make a mistake, click on the Undo button on the toolbar shown in Figure 8.4. This will undo your last action. You can use it several times to undo a series of actions. If you undo too many times, click on the Redo button which will carry out the action you removed with undo.

e. Figure 8.4 shows my leaflet design. Explore the other designs by clicking on the Publication Designs option, and scroll down the box.

Undo Redo

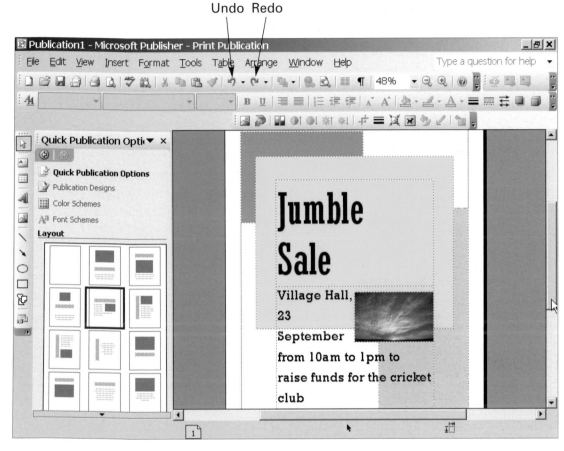

Figure 8.4 Leaflet

f. Print your leaflet when you are satisfied with the design.

g. Close Microsoft Publisher® using the File menu and Exit option.

h. Switch off the computer using the correct procedure.

2. Improve your efforts

> **ICT Skill for Life standard**
>
> This task helps you to practise:
>
> - entering information, formatting text, checking meaning, accuracy and suitability
> - presenting information that is fit for a purpose.

In Chapter 5, you produced a short notice (see page 76). In this task you are going to improve its presentation. One of the major advantages of word processors is that you can edit your work and improve it.

a. Switch on the computer and open Microsoft Word® and load the notice you worked on in Chapter 5.

b. Consider your earlier efforts. For example:

> If you are the last person to leave, please check that all the windows are shut and the lights have been turned off.

or

> On Saturday 23 September we have organised a trip to Chatsworth House. If you would like to take part, please contact Dorothy.

c. Improve the presentation of your notice by adding a bold heading to draw people's attention to the message. Change the font and character size so that it is easy to read. Add a date and name to the notice to make it look official (see Figure 8.5).

d. Carefully read your notice and correct any errors using the 'Backspace' and 'Delete' keys.

e. Use the Spelling and Grammar checker.

f. Print the notice by selecting the File menu, Print option and OK button.

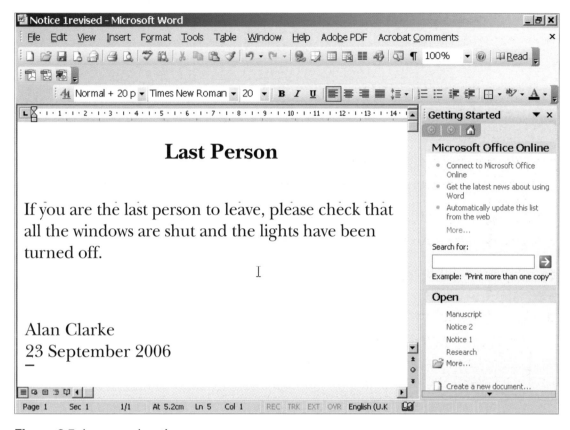

Figure 8.5 Improved notice

g. Save your revised notice using <u>F</u>ile menu and the <u>S</u>ave option to open the 'Save As' window. Give the notice a meaningful file name such as 'Notice Revised'.

h. Close Microsoft Word® using the <u>F</u>ile menu and the E<u>x</u>it option.

i. Switch off the computer using the correct procedure.

Economic activity, including paid and unpaid work

1. Things-to-do list

> **ICT Skill for Life standard**
>
> This task helps you to practise:
>
> - entering information using copy, cut, paste, drag and drop, undo and redo to achieve the required outcome
>
> - aligning and justifying text
>
> - bringing together information to achieve a purpose
>
> - checking meaning, accuracy and suitability
>
> - presenting information that is fit for a purpose.

Life is very busy and it is difficult to remember everything that you need to do. Many people find writing a list useful. It reminds them of each task.

a. Switch on the computer and open Microsoft Word®.

b. Consider how to present the list so that it is most effective. If everything is clear, you will not miss an item.

c. Figure 8.6 shows an example of one of my lists. I have used a large character size for the heading, numbered each item, and left a blank line between each item so the items can be easily seen.

d. Carefully read your list and correct any errors using the 'Backspace' and 'Delete' keys.

e. Use the Spelling and Grammar checker.

f. Print the list by selecting the File menu and clicking on the Print option. This will open the 'Print' window. Click on the OK button to start printing the list.

g. Save your list by selecting the File menu and clicking on the Save option. This will open the 'Save As' window where you can enter a meaningful file name such as 'Things to do list'.

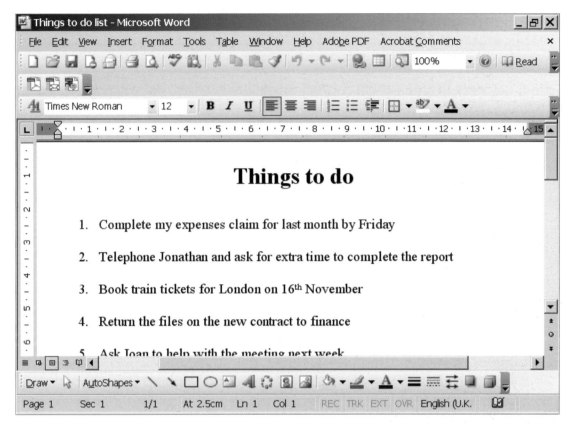

Figure 8.6 List

h. Close Microsoft Word® by selecting the <u>F</u>ile menu and clicking on the E<u>x</u>it option.

i. Switch off the computer using the correct procedure.

2. Presenting numbers

ICT Skill for Life standard

This task helps you to practise:

- entering and processing numbers
- aligning and justifying text
- bringing together information to achieve a purpose
- checking meaning, accuracy and suitability
- presenting information that is fit for a purpose.

Many jobs involve working with numbers. Spreadsheets are designed to help with this.

a. Switch on the computer and open Microsoft Excel®.

b. Consider a task that involves presenting a table of numbers.

c. Figure 8.7 shows an example of a table. It is an aid to calculating the cost of multiple items. It shows the VAT (value added tax) and delivery costs separately. The headings are emboldened and each column is centred. The costs were calculated using a calculator. For example:

Cost of item = 5.55 × number of items

VAT = Cost of item × 0.175

Total = Cost + VAT + Delivery

d. Carefully read and check your work. You can correct any errors by clicking in the cell and entering the information again.

e. Use the Spelling and Grammar checker.

f. Print the table by selecting the File menu and clicking on the Print option. This will open the 'Print' window. Click on the OK button to start printing the table.

	Microsoft Excel - Number table								_ □ ×

File   Edit   View   Insert   Format   Tools   Data   Window   Help   Adobe PDF   Type a question for help   ▼ _ ₽ ×

	A	B	C	D	E	F	G	H	I
1									
2			Items	Cost	VAT	Delivery	Total		
3			1	5.55	0.97	10	16.52		
4			2	11.10	1.94	10	23.04		
5			3	16.65	2.91	10	29.56		
6			4	22.20	3.89	10	36.09		
7			5	27.75	4.86	10	42.61		
8			6	33.30	5.83	10	49.13		
9			7	38.85	6.80	10	55.65		
10			8	44.40	7.77	10	62.17		
11			9	49.95	8.74	10	68.69		
12			10	55.50	9.71	10	75.21		
13									
14									
15									

Sheet1 / Sheet2 / Sheet3 /

Ready

Figure 8.7 Numbers table

g. Save your table by selecting the File menu and clicking on the Save option. This will open the 'Save As' window where you can enter a meaningful file name such as 'Number Table'.

h. Close Microsoft Excel® by selecting the File menu and clicking on the Exit option.

i. Switch off the computer using the correct procedure.

Domestic and everyday life

1. Write a letter of complaint

> ### ICT Skill for Life standard
>
> This task helps you to practise:
>
> - entering information using copy, cut, paste, drag and drop, undo and redo to achieve the required outcome
>
> - aligning and justifying text
>
> - bringing together information to achieve a purpose
>
> - checking meaning, accuracy and suitability
>
> - presenting information that is fit for a purpose.

There may be an occasion when you need to complain. Writing a letter of complaint using a word processor allows you to keep a copy that you can then use in the future. Figure 8.8 shows an example complaint letter.

a. Switch on the computer and open Microsoft Word®.

b. Consider a problem or issue that you would like to complain about.

c. Using the word processor, write a short letter showing:

    i. the address of the person you are sending the letter to

    ii. your own address

    iii. the date and your full name.

d. Choose a font type and character size that you feel is appropriate and embolden the heading.

e. Correct any mistakes using the 'Backspace' and 'Delete' keys or the Undo and Redo functions.

f. Use the Spelling and Grammar checker.

g. Carefully check your final letter for meaning and accuracy.

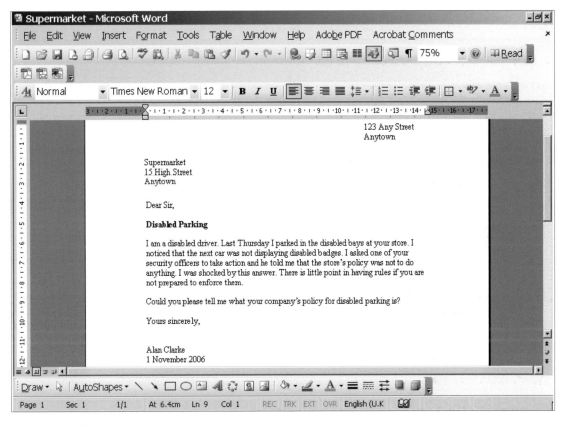

Figure 8.8 Complaint letter

h. Print a copy of the letter by selecting the File menu and clicking on the Print option. This will open the 'Print' window. Click on the OK button to start printing the letter.

i. Save your table by selecting the File menu and clicking on the Save option. This will open the 'Save As' window where you can enter a suitable name such as 'Supermarket'.

j. Close Microsoft Word® by selecting the File menu and clicking on the Exit option.

k. Switch off the computer using the correct procedure.

2. Create a party invitation

> ### ICT Skill for Life standard
>
> This task helps you to practise:
>
> - entering information using copy, cut, paste, drag and drop, undo and redo to achieve the required outcome
>
> - aligning and justifying text
>
> - inserting and positioning images to achieve a purpose
>
> - bringing together information to achieve a purpose
>
> - checking meaning, accuracy and suitability
>
> - presenting information that is fit for a purpose.

Pictures can create attractive and eye-catching documents.

a. Switch on the computer and open the Microsoft Word® application.

b. Design an invitation to a party or event that you are organising. Figure 8.9 shows my invitation. I have used different character sizes to emphasise the message, and enclosed the words in a red border.

The details of my invitation are:

- 'Invitation' uses a bold 36 character size and is centred

- 'Alan's Birthday Party' uses a bold 24 character size and is centred

- 'On: 13th February 2007' uses a bold 18 character size and is left aligned

- 'At: 8pm' uses a bold 18 character size and is left aligned

- '111 Any Street, Anytown' uses a bold 16 character size and is centred

- 'RSVP' uses a bold 16 character size and is right aligned.

c. Correct any mistakes on your invitation using the 'Backspace' and 'Delete' keys or the Undo and Redo functions.

d. Use the Spelling and Grammar checker.

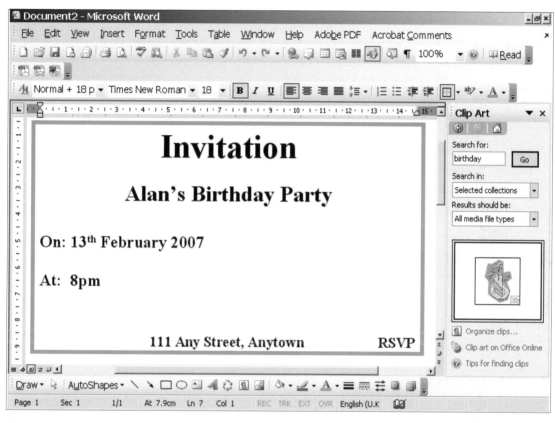

Figure 8.9 Invitation

e. Insert a clip art image into the invitation. To select a clip art image, use the Insert menu and highlight the Picture option to reveal the sub-menu. Click on the Clip Art option. This will open the 'Clip Art' task pane. Figure 8.9 shows the open task pane. This lets you search for an image by entering a search word such as 'birthday' and clicking on the Go button. The search will show you images that match your search word. If you double-click on the image then it will be imported into the invitation.

Vocab

Clip art is a collection of images that you can choose from.

Task pane is a window that opens when a function such as clip art is opened. Figure 8.9 shows an open 'Clip Art' task pane.

Import means to transfer the image into your document.

f. The clip art image needs to be positioned by dragging with the mouse and mouse pointer.

g. Carefully check your invitation for meaning and accuracy.

h. Print a copy of the invitation by selecting the <u>F</u>ile menu and clicking on the <u>P</u>rint option. This will open the 'Print' window. Click on the OK button to start printing the invitation.

i. Save the invitation file by selecting the <u>F</u>ile menu and clicking on the <u>S</u>ave option. This will open the 'Save As' window where you can enter a suitable name such as 'Invitation'.

j. Close Microsoft Word® by selecting the <u>F</u>ile menu and clicking on the E<u>x</u>it option.

k. Switch off the computer using the correct procedure.

Leisure

1. Catalogue a collection

> **ICT Skill for Life standard**
>
> This task helps you to practise:
>
> - entering information using copy, cut, paste, drag and drop, undo and redo to achieve the required outcome
>
> - aligning and justifying text
>
> - bringing together information to achieve a purpose
>
> - checking meaning, accuracy and suitability
>
> - presenting information that is fit for a purpose.

Lots of people have collections such as stamps, music, postcards, dolls and so on. It is often useful to catalogue collections because this lets you know what you own and helps you to identify any gaps in your collection. Cataloguing may also be useful if you need to make an insurance claim.

a. Consider your collection. How would you describe an individual item? This will help you to decide how to lay out the catalogue of the collection. For example, a collection of picture postcards could be catalogued using the following descriptions:

    i. publisher

    ii. picture

    iii. date

    iv. value.

b. Switch on the computer and open the Microsoft Word® application.

c. Design a catalogue layout and enter five items. Figure 8.10 shows my catalogue.

    My layout is:

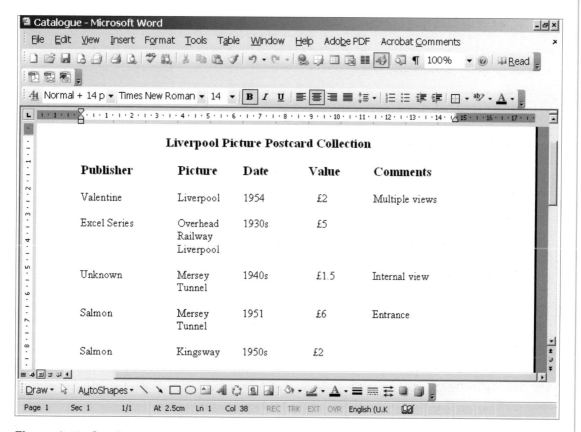

Figure 8.10 Catalogue

- ■ 'Liverpool Picture Postcard Collection' uses a bold size 14 character and is centred.
- ■ 'Publisher', 'Picture', 'Date', 'Value' and 'Comments' headings use a bold size 14 character and are laid out across the page.
- ■ Other text uses a size 12 character.

d. Correct any mistakes in your catalogue layout using the 'Backspace' and 'Delete' keys or the Undo and Redo functions.

e. Use the Spelling and Grammar checker.

f. Carefully check your catalogue for meaning and accuracy. Cut, copy, paste, and drag and drop entries so that the items are in alphabetical order. Figure 8.11 shows my catalogue in alphabetical order.

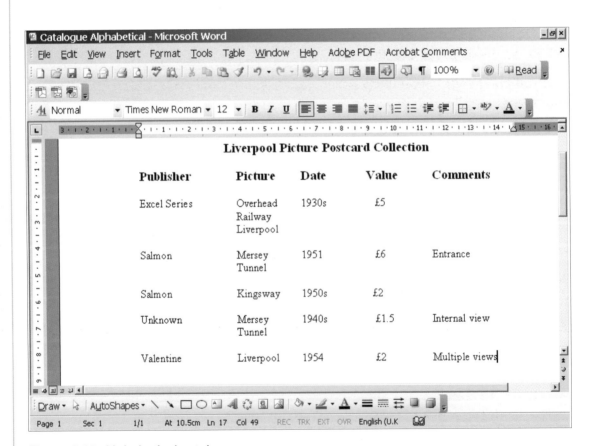

Figure 8.11 Alphabetical catalogue

g. Print a copy of the catalogue by selecting the <u>F</u>ile menu and clicking on the <u>P</u>rint option. This will open the 'Print' window. Click on the OK button to start printing the catalogue.

h. Save the catalogue file by selecting the <u>F</u>ile menu and clicking on the <u>S</u>ave option. This will open the 'Save As' window where you can enter a suitable name such as 'Catalogue'.

i. Close Microsoft Word® by selecting the <u>F</u>ile menu and clicking on the E<u>x</u>it option.

j. Switch off the computer using the correct procedure.

2. Create an answer sheet for a quiz

> **ICT Skill for Life standard**
>
> This task helps you to practise:
>
> - entering information using copy, cut, paste, drag and drop, undo and redo to achieve the required outcome
>
> - aligning and justifying text
>
> - bringing together information to achieve a purpose
>
> - checking meaning, accuracy and suitability
>
> - presenting information that is fit for purpose.

Quizzes are very popular. They are often used to raise funds for a good cause or simply as entertainment. This task helps you to design and create an answer sheet for a general knowledge quiz.

a. Think about the type of quiz for which the sheet will be used. This will help you to design the answer sheet.

Example answer sheet plan

    i. Each team needs to have a name.

    ii. There are five rounds of questions.

iii. Each round will have three questions except round four.

iv. Round four is a picture question where teams have to identify five photographs of people.

v. The quiz master needs to be able to add marks to the answer sheet and produce a total.

b. Switch on the computer and open the Microsoft Word® application.

c. Design an answer sheet. Figure 8.12 shows my answer sheet design.

My layout is:

■ 'Answer Sheet' uses a bold size 20 character and is centred.

■ 'Team' uses a bold size 16 character and is centred.

■ A dotted line after 'Team' allows the team's name to be added.

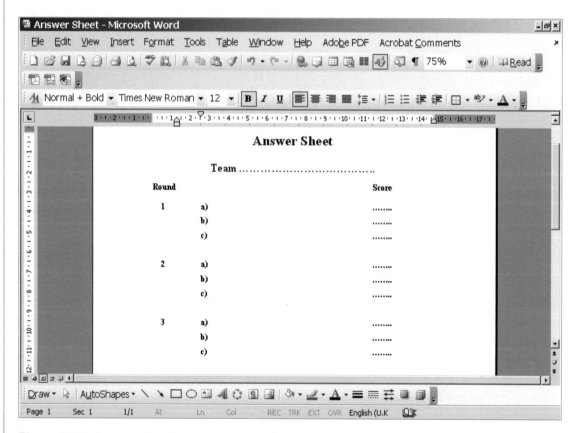

Figure 8.12 Answer sheet

- ■ 'Round' and 'Score' are positioned to allow space for answers to be inserted.

- ■ 'Round' and 'Score' use a bold size 12 character.

- ■ Other text uses a bold size 12 character.

d. On your answer sheet, correct any mistakes using the 'Backspace' and 'Delete' keys or the Undo and Redo functions.

e. Use the Spelling and Grammar checker.

f. Carefully check your answer sheet to ensure it is fit for its purpose. If you need to change the layout, use the copy, cut, paste, and drag and drop functions.

g. Print a copy of the answer sheet by selecting the File menu and clicking on the Print option. This will open the 'Print' window. Click on the OK button to start printing the answer sheet.

h. Save the answer sheet by selecting the File menu and clicking on the Save option. This will open the 'Save As' window where you can enter a suitable name such as 'Answer Sheet'.

i. Close Microsoft Word® by selecting the File menu and clicking on the Exit option.

j. Switch off the computer using the correct procedure.

Education and training

1. Creating revision aids

ICT Skill for Life standard

This task helps you to practise:

- ■ entering information using copy, cut, paste, drag and drop, undo and redo to achieve the required outcome

- ■ aligning and justifying text

- ■ bringing together information achieve a purpose

- ■ checking meaning, accuracy and suitability

- ■ presenting information that is fit for a purpose.

When you are preparing for a test, it is useful to have some revision aids. These are simple summaries of the key points of the topics you have studied.

a. Switch on the computer and open the Microsoft Word® application.

b. Effective revision aids are often short and straightforward. They present the key points of a topic so that you can quickly revise them before a test. Figure 8.13 shows a revision aid for the battle of Waterloo.

c. Design a revision aid for a subject that you or one of your family is studying. Try to identify ten key points and enter them into Microsoft Word®.

d. Correct any mistakes using the 'Backspace' and 'Delete' keys or the Undo and Redo functions.

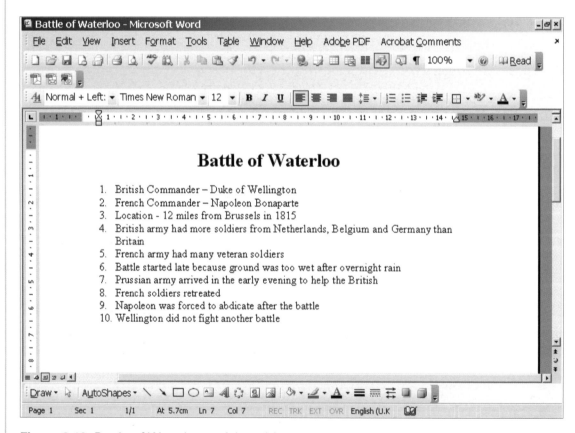

Figure 8.13 Battle of Waterloo revision aid

e. Use the <u>S</u>pelling and Grammar checker.

f. Carefully check your revision aid for meaning, and make sure it will help you to revise. If you need to change the layout, use the copy, cut, paste, and drag and drop functions.

g. Print a copy of the aid by selecting the <u>F</u>ile menu and clicking on the <u>P</u>rint option. This will open the 'Print' window. Click on the OK button to start printing the aid. Ask a friend or colleague to check it. Make any corrections that are needed.

h. Save the revision aid file by selecting the <u>F</u>ile menu and clicking on the Save option. This will open the 'Save As' window where you can enter a suitable name such as 'Battle of Waterloo'.

i. Close Microsoft Word® by selecting the <u>F</u>ile menu and clicking on the E<u>x</u>it option.

j. Switch off the computer using the correct procedure.

2. Adding pictures to an assignment

ICT Skill for Life standard

This task helps you to practise:

■ inserting and positioning images to achieve a purpose.

A picture is often said to be worth a thousand words. Adding images to an assignment will often enhance your presentation. This task helps you to use pictures to add interest to an education or training assignment that you or one of your friends is producing.

a. Switch on the computer and open the Microsoft Word® application.

b. You can add pictures from several sources to a document you are creating using Microsoft Word®. Figure 8.14 shows the menus and options. The options are:

■ 'Clip Art' – pictures from clip art

■ 'From File' – pictures saved as a file in a folder

- 'From Scanner or Camera' – pictures from a digital camera or scanner.

c. Explore the different options and add a picture to your document. I chose to add an image from my scanner. Figure 8.15 shows part of the process of adjusting the image that will appear in your document. Figure 8.16 shows the image imported into the document.

Vocab

A **scanner** is a device that allows you to copy a picture or text into a computer application.

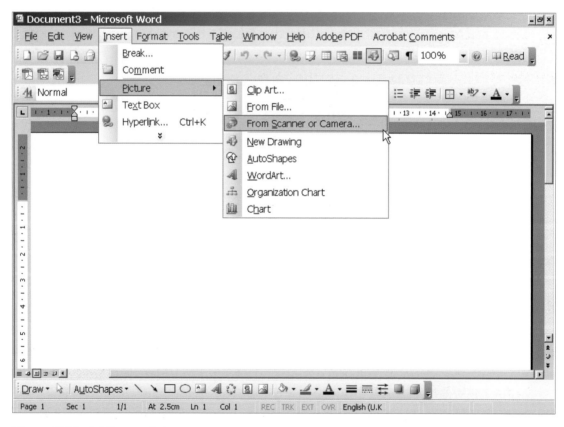

Figure 8.14 Adding a picture

Pointer changing
scanned image shape

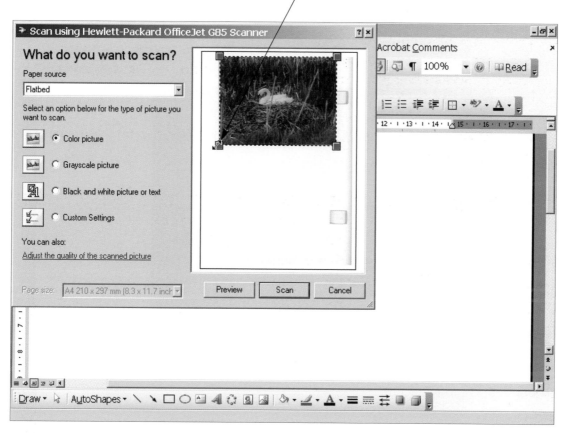

Figure 8.15 Scanning a photograph

d. On your document, correct any mistakes using the Undo and Redo functions.

e. Print a copy of your document by selecting the File menu and clicking on the Print option. This will open the 'Print' window. Click on the OK button to start printing the document.

f. Save the document by selecting the File menu and clicking on the Save option. This will open the 'Save As' window where you can enter a suitable name.

Figure 8.16 Imported picture

g. Close Microsoft Word® by selecting the File menu and clicking on the Exit option.

h. Switch off the computer using the correct procedure.

Summary

Here are some useful tasks for you to do:

- Practise entering text and number information into different applications such as Microsoft Word®, Publisher®, Excel® and Windows Paint®.

- Practise using techniques such as copying, cutting, pasting, dragging and dropping, and undoing and redoing.

- Practise aligning, justifying and formatting text.

- Practise inserting and positioning images.

- Practise entering and processing numbers.

- Practise bringing different types of information together to achieve a purpose.

- Always check your work for meaning, accuracy and suitability.

- Always consider the purpose of the work you are creating.

9 Assessment

Introduction

This book is based on the ICT Skill for Life standards that provide the foundation for the ICT Skill for Life qualifications. Three of the awarding bodies that have developed ICT Skill for Life qualifications are:

- OCR
- City and Guilds
- Edexcel.

Other awarding bodies have also produced awards, but these are not included in this book.

All three sets of qualifications recognise that all learners will have individual needs that need to be addressed by their courses. The courses are expected to follow the ICT Skill for Life curriculum. However, each awarding body has specified the assessment requirements to achieve its qualification. Please discuss with your tutor the assessment for the qualification you are studying.

OCR

The assessment is based on OCR assignments that are undertaken at the centre where you are studying. You need to meet all the assessment requirements fully by gathering the evidence that is detailed in the assignment. Evidence will often take the form of a print-out to show that you have completed a task. The staff at the centre will mark the evidence and offer you an opportunity to fill any gaps left in the evidence. When the centre is satisfied that you have met the entire requirement, it will send the evidence to OCR for moderation. This ensures that standards are being maintained at all centres.

The OCR ICT Skill for Life qualification is divided into several units:

1. One unit called 'Using ICT systems' (Entry Level 1)

2. Three units called 'Displaying information using ICT', 'Using ICT to find information' and 'Communicating information using ICT' (Entry Level 2)

3. Three units called 'Displaying information using ICT', 'Using ICT to find information' and 'Communicating information using ICT' (Entry Level 3).

To achieve the full OCR Entry Level Certificate, you must pass all the units at the level you are studying. However, a unit certificate is awarded for each unit passed. Figure 9.1 shows how each of the OCR units aligns with the ICT Skill for Life standard.

The OCR units combine to cover the ICT Skill for Life standard. You should discuss the assessment requirements for your qualification with your tutor. The following section is only intended to provide you with a flavour of the assessment tasks you need to complete.

OCR units	ICT Skill for Life standards
Entry Level 1: Using ICT systems	This unit covers the whole Entry Level 1 standard
Entry Level 2A: Displaying information using ICT	This unit covers the whole standard for 'Developing and presenting information', plus some aspects of 'Using ICT systems'
Entry Level 2B: Using ICT to find information	This unit covers aspects of 'Using ICT systems', 'Finding and exchanging information' and 'Developing and presenting information'
Entry Level 2C: Communicating information using ICT	This unit covers aspects of 'Using ICT systems', 'Finding and exchanging information' and 'Developing and presenting information'
Entry Level 3A: Displaying information using ICT	This unit covers the whole standard for 'Developing and presenting information' plus most aspects of 'Using ICT systems'
Entry Level 3B: Using ICT to find information	This unit covers aspects of 'Using ICT systems' and most aspects of 'Finding and exchanging information'
Entry Level 3C: Communicating information using ICT	This unit covers aspects of 'Using ICT systems', 'Finding and exchanging information', and 'Developing and presenting information'

Figure 9.1 OCR units and standards

Assessment

Entry Level 1: Using ICT systems

At this level, you need to show that you can find information from an ICT-based system that your tutor opens for you. This could involve reading information displayed on a computer screen. You need to receive an ICT-based communication, for example a text message. Finally, you have to access a computer system such as a cash machine.

The evidence required is that your tutor witnesses these activities being successfully completed.

Entry Level 2

Entry Level 2A: Displaying information using ICT

For this unit, you need to enter some words and numbers to produce a short document. You should check your work and save it with the help of your tutor.

The evidence required is a print-out of your document or a witness statement from your tutor.

Entry Level 2B: Using ICT to find information

For this unit, you must find two pieces of information from different sources, for example a website and a DVD.

The evidence required is print-outs of the information or your own notes of the information found.

Entry Level 2C: Communicating information using ICT

For this unit, you need to send and receive two messages, for example emails.

The evidence required is print-outs of the messages.

Entry Level 3

Entry Level 3A: Displaying information using ICT

For this unit, you have to create a document for your own purpose, for example a leaflet, letter or invitation. The document should contain words, numbers and a picture. You should check your work, print and save it. The document file should then be retrieved and the formatting changed. It should now be reprinted and saved again.

The evidence required is the print-outs of the two documents.

Entry Level 3B: Using ICT to find information

For this unit, you need to undertake two searches from different sources, for example the World Wide Web and a DVD. You need to detail what information you are trying to find.

The evidence required is print-outs of the information or your own notes of the information found.

Entry Level 3C: Communicating information using ICT

For this unit, you must demonstrate your skills in using email. You need to create, receive, open, delete and reply to emails.

The evidence required is print-outs of the messages that you have sent, received and replied to.

City and Guilds

The assessment is based on carrying out an assignment provided by City and Guilds. The centre where you are studying will present the assignment to you and mark your efforts. The national standards are maintained from a system of internal and external checking.

City and Guilds provides three qualifications:

1. Entry Level Certificate in ICT Skill for Life (Entry 1)
2. Entry Level Certificate in ICT Skill for Life (Entry 2)
3. Entry Level Certificate in ICT Skill for Life (Entry 3).

These align with the ICT Skill for Life standards at each level.

The assignments are provided in the context of the five ICT Skill for Life areas (see page 2). You should find that one of the assignments relates to your interests and needs. The assignments are intended to provide a set of actions that enables the standard to be assessed at each level.

Assessment

The examples shown are simply intended to illustrate some possible assignments. You should discuss the actual assessment assignments with your tutor.

Entry Level 1

At this level, your tutor will switch on the computer and open any application that you need. You will be asked to enter some simple information from the keyboard and to make some choices.

Entry Level 2

At this level, you will switch on the computer and enter a password to gain access to the system. You will be asked to open and use any application that you need. You will be asked to enter and check information that you have entered from the keyboard and to make some choices. Finally, you will be required to print your work.

Entry Level 3

At this level, you will switch on the computer and enter a password to gain access to the system. You will be asked to open and use any application that you need. You will be asked to enter, edit and check information that you have entered from the keyboard. Editing will involve making changes to the format of information and using a spell checker. You will save and print your work. The final step will be to close the application and switch off the computer system.

Edexcel

The assessment is undertaken using Edexcel designed activities. These are intended to provide purposeful activities in line with the ICT Skill for Life standard. The centre where you are studying will present the assessment to you when you are ready, and it will mark your efforts. The national standards are maintained from a system of internal and external checking.

The assessment activities cover the whole entry level so that activities cover all three areas of the standard. That is:

1. Using ICT systems (Entry Level 1)
2. Finding and exchanging information (Entry Level 2)
3. Developing and presenting information (Entry Level 3).

The assessment will consist of at least:

- one on-screen skills-based activity
- one knowledge-based activity
- a task-based activity.

The on-screen activities are marked by the computer and the task-based activity is marked by your centre staff.

Edexcel offers three qualifications:

1. Entry Level 1 Certificate in Adult ICT

2. Entry Level 2 Certificate in Adult ICT

3. Entry Level 3 Certificate in Adult ICT.

These align with the ICT Skill for Life standards at each level.

Assessment

The examples shown are simply intended to illustrate some possible activities. They are not intended to provide the whole assessment at each level. You should discuss the actual assessment activities with your tutor.

Entry Level 1

At this level you may be asked to:

- enter simple information into a computer system, for example your name, a password or a PIN
- identify appropriate sources of information, for example a website or road map
- click on a button.

Entry Level 2

At this level you may be asked to:

- use a computer application such as a word processor or an online form
- enter brief details into a computer application, for example your name and address
- check your entry for accuracy and make any required corrections.

Entry Level 3

At this level you may be asked to:

■ reply to an email

■ create a leaflet

■ amend a document.

Summary

Entry Level 1

The ICT Skill for Life standard places an emphasis on you being able to:

a. interact with ICT safely, for example by receiving a text message

b. identify sources and get information from them, for example by reading an electronic display

c. enter and edit information for a purpose, for example by entering a password to gain access to the computer system.

Entry Level 2

The ICT Skill for Life standard places an emphasis on you being able to:

a. interact and use ICT safely and securely for a purpose, for example by browsing a website

b. find and use ICT-based sources of information, for example by searching a CD-ROM

c. use ICT to communicate, for example by sending an email

d. enter and edit information for a purpose, for example by word-processing a short note

▶

ICT SKILL FOR LIFE

e. present information for a purpose, for example an invitation

f. check and correct any errors.

Entry Level 3

The ICT Skill for Life standard places an emphasis on you being able to:

a. interact and use ICT safely and securely for a purpose, for example by creating a poster

b. select and use appropriate sources of information, for example by finding and printing directions for a journey

c. search for and use information that matches requirements, for example by using a search engine to locate information about a holiday location

d. access and use ICT to communicate, for example by opening an email system to receive, reply to and send emails

e. enter and develop information to suit a purpose, for example by entering text, numbers and images to create a poster

f. present information in ways that are fit for a purpose, for example by formatting a job application letter.

10 Individual development

Introduction

ICT is a dynamic subject. New technologies and new versions of existing computer applications are continually being developed. If you want to keep and build on your skills, understanding and knowledge of ICT, it is important to continue to study and take advantage of any learning opportunities. This chapter offers some suggestions for practical tasks that you can undertake to develop yourself. All the tasks are suitable for Entry Level 3.

Self-development

Many ICT users develop their own skills by taking advantage of opportunities to try new computer applications, systems and hardware. Although many applications and new equipment may appear different, they are often based on familiar systems and ideas. For example, controls will almost always be shown as icons or within menus. It is normal to offer more than one way of carrying out a task. You can select the icon or open the menu. The key is to explore the new application or equipment.

Transfer

It is important to be able to transfer your understanding and skills of one computer application or piece of equipment to new situations. Applications and operating systems have functions and features that operate in identical or very similar ways. You can also change the settings of operating systems to make it appear like the one you have been using.

Display

The Microsoft Windows® operating system allows you to customise its appearance. In order to change the display setting, use the Display function in the Control Panel. Figure 6.10 (page 107) shows the 'Control Panel'. If you click on the Display icon, the window shown in Figure 10.1 will appear. The 'Display' window has a series of tabs across the top that gives access to a range of functions:

- 'Themes'
- 'Desktop'
- 'Screen Saver'
- 'Appearance'
- 'Settings'.

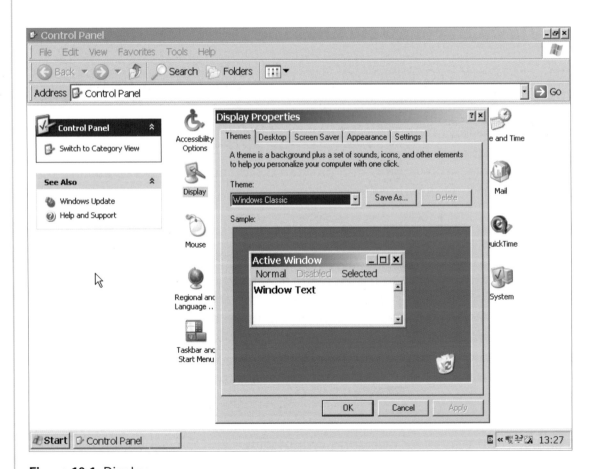

Figure 10.1 Display

Task 1 Entry Level 3: ICT user skills

Use the Display function in the Control Panel and explore the options by selecting different ones and watching the changes. To return to the previous settings, repeat the action and choose the original setting. It is worth making a note of this before you start. For example:

ICT Skill for Life standard

This task helps you to:

■ understand that settings can be adjusted according to individual needs.

a. Change the theme by clicking on the down arrow box and choosing from the list shown. Click on the OK button to start the change.

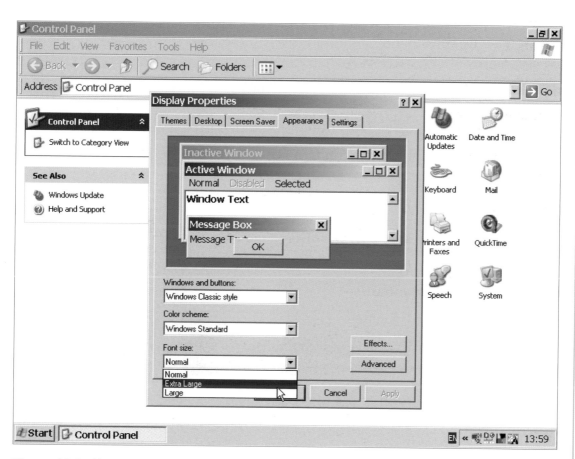

Figure 10.2 'Appearance' tab display

b. Choose the Appearance tab. The result is shown in Figure 10.2. Change the font size to Extra Large and then click on the OK button.

Operating systems

There are several versions of the Microsoft Windows® operating system. When you move between different computers or change your job, you may find yourself using a computer with a different version of Microsoft Windows®. This can be confusing, but the different systems have lots of things in common. They will all have:

- a desktop
- a 'Start' button
- an 'All Programs menu', although this is sometimes simply called 'Programs'
- 'Accessories' with Microsoft Windows Paint®, Calculator and Windows Explorer®
- a 'Help and Support' option, sometimes just called 'Help'
- 'Control Panel' options leading to 'Display', 'Mouse' and 'Accessibility' options
- a 'Search' function.

Task 2 Entry Level 3: ICT user skills

> **ICT Skill for Life standard**
>
> This task helps you to practise:
>
> - recognising and using interface features.

When using a new version of the Microsoft Windows® operating system, spend a few minutes locating the functions listed above and familiarising yourself with the system.

Applications

There are many functions available across all the Microsoft Office® applications. These include:

- 'Save'
- 'Save as'
- 'Print'
- 'Cut', 'Copy' and 'Paste'
- 'Bold', 'Underline' and 'Italics'
- 'Alignment'.

Task 3 Entry Level 3: ICT user skills

ICT Skill for Life standard

This task helps you to practise:

- recognising and using interface features
- using software applications to achieve a purpose.

a. Compare the different applications that you have used. Figures 3.4 and 3.5 show Microsoft Word® and Excel®. Their displays are very similar, both having:

- 'File', 'Edit', 'View', 'Insert', 'Format', 'Tools', 'Window' and 'Help' options along the menu bar.

b. Compare the different Microsoft Word® and Excel® menus and again you will see similar options. Figure 10.3 shows the Microsoft Word® 'Edit' menu and Figure 10.4 the Microsoft Excel® 'Edit' menu.

c. Since the applications have just been opened in Figures 10.3 and 10.4, they both show a task pane on the right called 'Getting Started'. Review the different options in this task pane.

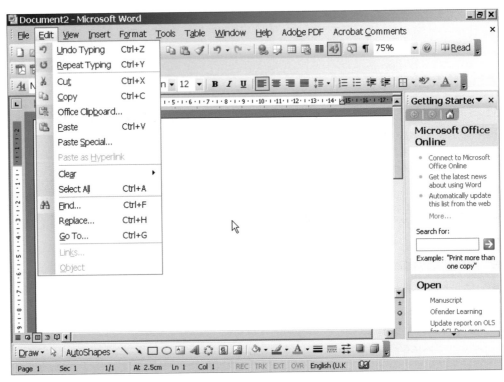

Figure 10.3 Microsoft Word® 'Edit' menu

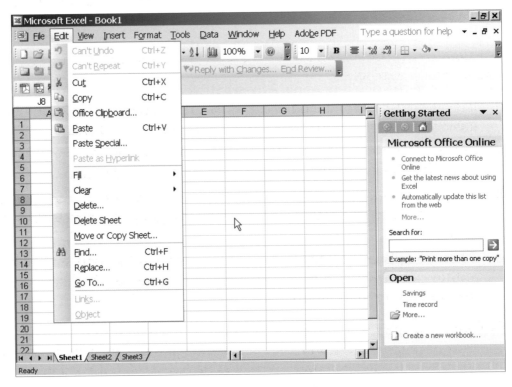

Figure 10.4 Microsoft Excel® 'Edit' menu

Techniques

Many common techniques are available in most ICT applications or systems. These techniques include:

- pointer
- highlighting
- left and right mouse buttons
- links
- drag and drop
- double-clicking
- single-clicking.

Pointer

The mouse pointer serves several purposes. If you simply place the pointer over an icon or other object, it will often reveal a small label explaining its function. Figure 10.5 illustrates the label.

The pointer will sometimes simply change shape. This provides you with clues about what is available.

1. In Microsoft Word®, the pointer will take the shape of an 'I' bar in the work area. This shows you that text can be inputted into this area.
2. In Microsoft Excel®, the pointer will take the shape of a '+' sign in the work area. This shows you that numbers and words can be entered.
3. The pointer changes to a hand when it is over a link on a website. This indicates that if you click the mouse, you can jump to a new section of the website.
4. When you place the pointer over a menu or other function, it is highlighted to show you what you activate if you click the mouse. This helps to ensure that you do not make mistakes.

Explore the display with the pointer. It can provide you with a lot of useful information. Figures 10.3 and 10.4 show the pointer as an arrow shape. In Figure 10.5, the pointer shows a label, and in Figure 10.6 the pointer is in the shape of a hand to show a link.

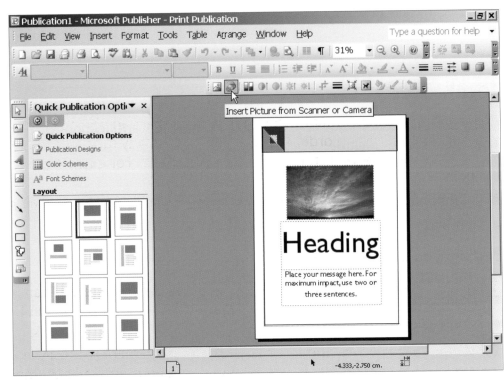

Figure 10.5 Using a pointer in Microsoft Publisher®

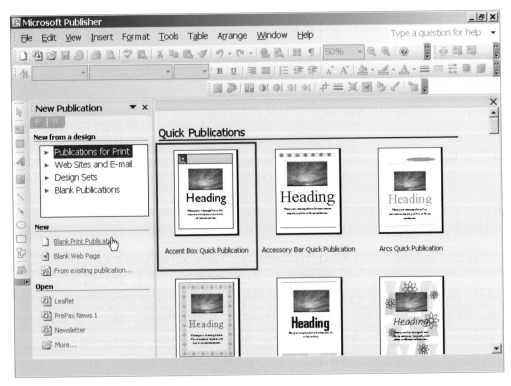

Figure 10.6 Pointer showing a link

Highlighting

Highlighting is an important technique that identifies an object, such as a word or a spreadsheet cell, in order to make a change. Many functions operate on a highlighted word or object, for instance 'Alignment'. For example:

Highlight a sentence in order to centre align it using the Centered alignment option.

Highlighting can take two main forms:

1. When text and numbers are highlighted, the background and foreground colours reverse. Figure 5.2 (page 73) provides an example of text being highlighted.
2. When images, icons and interface features are highlighted, they are enclosed in a rectangle. Figure 10.6 provides an example of an image being enclosed.

Left and right mouse buttons

When you click on an icon or option in order to choose it, you use the left mouse button. However, in some cases, if you click with the right button another menu of options appears. Figure 10.7 shows a right mouse button menu in Microsoft Word®.

The menu shown in Figure 10.7 has several useful options such as 'Cut', 'Copy', 'Paste', 'Font' and 'Bullets and Numbering'.

Links

Links are sometimes called 'hyperlinks'. They allow you to move between different parts of a website or between websites. Links are often shown by a word being underlined or by the mouse pointer changing shape when it moves over the word. Links can be to completely different websites, between

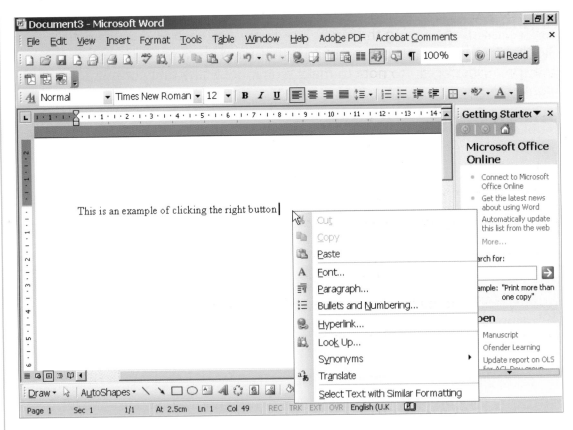

Figure 10.7 Right mouse button menu

different pages of one website, or simply around a specific web page. When you next visit a website, try to find:

- the different types of links, for example an underlined word or a picture
- where the link takes you to, for example a different website, a different page within the website or another part of the web page.

Drag and drop, double-clicking and single-clicking

These techniques relate to using the mouse pointer and buttons. Drag and drop is a way of moving words or pictures around and it is an alternative to cut and paste. You highlight the words or pictures by holding down the left mouse button. This allows you to drag them to a new position.

Double- and single-clicking are both used to make choices on screen. Double-clicking involves pressing the left mouse button twice, as fast as you can. Single-clicking is simply pressing the left mouse button once. When you are using a computer, try to notice when you need to click once or twice.

Task 4 Entry Level 3: ICT user skills

ICT Skill for Life standard

This task helps you to practise:

- recognising and using interface features
- using software applications to achieve a purpose.

Use the right mouse button and see what menu options appear.

Summary

Here are some useful tasks for you to do:

- Compare the options in different Microsoft Windows® operating systems.
- Practise changing the settings in the Microsoft Windows® operating system.
- Compare the options in different computer applications.
- Observe how the mouse pointer changes shape and how it reveals information.
- Use the right mouse button to see if additional options are revealed

Glossary

Accessibility – this is about making the computer system more suitable for people to use.

Accessories – accessories are extra applications that are included in a computer system.

Application – an application is a tool that allows you to carry out different tasks. A word processor helps you to write and present text.

Back button – an option in the top left-hand corner of Microsoft Internet Explorer® that allows you to retrace your steps between links.

Backspace – a key on the keyboard or calculator that deletes a character to the left of the cursor.

Bulletin board – a communication system where messages are sent to a website so that you can read them when you visit the site.

Button – an area of the display that you can click with the mouse. It will then start an action.

Cell – a cell is the area formed when spreadsheet rows and columns intersect. Figure 3.5 (page 28) shows the work area divided up into rows and columns to form a grid of cells in Microsoft Excel®.

Clip art – a collection of images that you can choose from.

Control Panel – a window in the Microsoft Windows® operating system. It provides ways to customise the computer system to your needs.

Cursor – when entering text using the keyboard, the cursor marks the place on screen where the new text will appear. It is often shown as a flashing bar.

Database – a collection of information stored on the computer in a way that makes it easy to find particular pieces of information.

Del – the shortened form of 'Delete' and a key on the keyboard.

Desktop – the main computer display is called the 'desktop'. Microsoft Windows® opens to show the desktop.

Domain – part of a website address. It is often the name of the website owner or provider.

Edit – to make changes, for example to remove part of a photograph or to change the spelling of a word.

Enter – 'enter' has several meanings including typing in information using the keyboard, and the name of a key or a button on a keyboard.

Eraser tool – essentially an electronic rubber that lets you rub out parts of a drawing. It is normally provided in graphics or Microsoft Windows Paint® applications.

Explore – 'explore' has several meanings including

Glossary

to try different options to see what they do.

File – a collection of information, for example a letter.

Fit for a purpose – suitable for the task you are doing.

Folder – a storage space to hold files.

Graphic – a picture, drawing or shape.

Hardware – the physical equipment that makes up a computer or other ICT.

Home page – the first page of a website.

Hotspot – an area in the website display that you can click on with the mouse and it takes you to another part of the website.

Icon – a small picture on the display screen.

Import – to transfer the contents of a file, such as an image, into a document.

Install – to copy instructions on to the computer so that it can read the information or application on a disk.

Interface – the parts of the computer system you use to communicate with the applications or operating system, for example the interface display, keyboard and mouse.

Interface display – what appears on the screen.

Interface features – the objects shown on the screen, for example icons, menus and buttons.

Input devices – pieces of equipment that let you enter information into ICT, for example a keyboard or a mouse.

Link – a connection between one part of a website and another.

Memory card – a small portable card on which information can be stored.

Menu – a list of options from which you can choose.

Monitor – a device that presents the computer's information. It resembles a television.

Mouse buttons – a mouse normally has two mouse buttons. You press the left button to confirm an action. The right button will open up new menus of options in some cases.

Mouse pointer – a small pointer that appears on the screen display and is controlled by moving the mouse.

Output devices – pieces of equipment that show the results of a task, for example a monitor or a printer.

Page – part of a website that presents information to you.

PC – the abbreviation for Personal Computer.

PIN – PIN is your Personal Identification Number for your credit or debit card.

Radio button – shows when an option is selected by

187

Glossary

placing a dot or tick in its centre. Figure 6.6 shows an example where 'Planning permission' is selected.

Required information – the information that you have been asked to find or that you need for your own purposes.

Requirements – 'requirements' has several meanings including your own needs.

Rows and columns – rows are the horizontal lines of information in a table. Columns are the vertical lines of information in a table (see Figure 2.2).

Scanner – a device that lets you copy a picture or text into a computer application.

Scroll – to move the display to the right and left or up and down. Scrolling is controlled by the scroll bars.

Search engine – a website that helps you to find web pages.

Search terms – words that you enter into a search engine when you want to find something on the internet. The words match the information you are looking for.

Site – a website on the World Wide Web.

SMS – Short Message Service, the official name for text messages or texts.

Software – the instructions that make the equipment work. Software is installed on the computer and you do not need to enter it.

Submit – to send information to the computer system so that it can act on it. Usually you press or click on a button.

Task pane – a window that opens when a function such as 'Clip Art' is opened. Figure 8.9 shows

an open 'Clip Art' task pane.

Using appropriate sources of ICT – choosing the correct ICT equipment and approach to achieve what you want, for example choosing the best way to send a message.

Using appropriate facilities – choosing the most suitable way to achieve what you want, for example choosing the best way to find the local weather forecast.

Web pages – sections of a website where information is displayed.

Windows® is the brand name of a major software product. However, a 'window' is also a rectangular area of the display that can be adjusted in size to cover the whole display or it can be reduced to an icon. Computer applications and information are shown in windows.

Index

Index

Index

Index